CAMBRIDGE IGCSE® DRAMA

Mike Gould and Rebekah Beattie

William Collins' dream of knowledge for all began with the publication of his first book in 1819. A self-educated mill worker, he not only enriched millions of lives, but also founded a flourishing publishing house. Today, staying true to this spirit, Collins books are packed with inspiration, innovation and practical expertise. They place you at the centre of a world of possibility and give you exactly what you need to explore it.

Collins. Freedom to teach

Published by Collins
An imprint of HarperCollins*Publishers*
The News Building
1 London Bridge Street
London SE1 9GF

© HarperCollins*Publishers* 2016

www.collins.co.uk

10 9 8 7 6 5 4 3 2 1

ISBN 978-0-00-812467-0

Publisher: **Celia Wigley**

Commissioning Editor: **Karen Jamieson**

Editor: **Hannah Dove**

Authors: **Mike Gould & Rebekah Beattie**

Copy-editor: **Hugh Hillyard-Parker**

Proof-reader: **Ros & Chris Davies**

Indexer: **Lisa Footitt**

Cover designer: **Gordon MacGilp & Angela English**

Permissions researcher: **Rachel Thorne**

Picture researcher: **Sophie Hartley**

Production controller: **Robin Forrester**

Typesetter: **Jouve India Private Limited**

Printed and bound in Italy by Grafica Veneta S. P. A.

IGCSE® is the registered trademark of Cambridge International Examinations

The publisher would like to thank the following for their assistance in the research for this book:

Ann Marie Cubbin, Brighton College, Dubai; Timothy Evans, The British International School, Phuket, Thailand; Robert Henson, Canggu Community School, Bali, Indonesia; Terry Nicholas, The International School of Cape Town, South Africa; James Russell, The International School of Brunei

Acknowledgements

Every effort has been made to trace copyright holders and to obtain their permission for the use of copyright material. The publishers will gladly receive any information enabling them to rectify any error or omission at the first opportunity.

The publishers would like to thank the following for permission to reproduce copyright material:

(t = top, b = bottom, c = centre, l = left, r = right)

Cover & p1 Jack.Q / Shutterstock, p7 leoks / Shutterstock, p8 B&Y Photography / Alamy, p8 Peter Brook, quote from *The Empty Space*, Penguin Classics, 2008, p11 keith morris / Alamy, p13 Roger Bamber / Alamy, p14 Pictorial Press Ltd / Alamy, p14 an extract from 'The Making of *Mandela: Long walk to freedom*' by Sally Williams, *The Daily Telegraph*, 07/12/2013, copyright © Telegraph Media Group Limited 2013, p16 Cultura RM Exclusive / Frank and Helena / Getty Images, p18l file404/ Shutterstock, p18r imagedb.com / Shutterstock, p20 Tristram Kenton / Royal Opera House / ArenaPAL, p20 an extract from *The Metamorphosis* by Franz Kafka, translated by Ian Johnston, 2011/01/08 copyright © Mauro Nervi, http://www.kafka.org/, p21l; p21r Antonio Guillem / Shutterstock, p25 Nigel Norrington / ArenaPAL, p26 dboystudio / Shutterstock, p28 Paul Doyle / Alamy, p29 Colin Willoughby / ArenaPAL, p29 an extract from *Sparkleshark* by Philip Ridley, published by Samuel French Ltd, 2000. Reprinted by permission of Samuel French Ltd, p30 William Frederick Yeames / Wikimedia Commons, p32t criben / Shutterstock, p32c aberCPC / Alamy, p32 an extract from *Sand Burial* by Mike Gould, copyright © Mike Gould, reproduced with non-exclusive permission, p34 Nigel Norrington / ArenaPAL, pp36–37 an extract from *Red Velvet* by Lolita Chakrabarti, Methuen Drama, 2012, pp57–58, copyright © Metheun, p35 Marilyn Kingwill / ArenaPAL, p41 T Charles Erickson, p42 an extract from *The House of Bernarda Alba* by Federico García Lorca, translated by Rona Munro, copyright © Nick Hern Books. Reproduced with permission, p43t Robbie Jack / Corbis, p43c; p44 Matt McArdle, p45 Captblack76 / Shutterstock, p46 Anna Bruce for the Pleasance Theatre Trust, p47c Kert / Shutterstock, p47b Andrea Pistolesi / Getty Images, p48t FashionStock.com / Shutterstock, p48c James Drawneek, p48b Ed Simons / Alamy Stock Photo, p49t Rebekah Beattie, p49b Mousetrap Production Company, pp50–51 an extract from *Amadeus* by Peter Shaffer, © HarperCollins, 1980, p52 Enigma / Alamy Stock Photo, p53l; p53c; p53r Steve Bree / Tom Kitney, at The Kings School Canterbury, p53b Wiskerke / Alamy Stock Photo, p54 an extract from *A Streetcar Named Desire* by Tennessee Williams, 1947. Reproduced by permission of Georges Borchardt Inc. and New Directions, p56 Petinov Sergey Mihilovich / Shutterstock, p57 kawing921 / Shutterstock, p58 Nigel Norrington / ArenaPAL, p59 an extract from *The Madness of George III* by Alan Bennett, © Faber & Faber, 1992, p60 Igor Bulgarin / Shutterstock, p61l Print Collector / Contributor / Getty Images, p61r Chris Jackson / Staff / Getty Images, p62cl Lars Zahner / Shutterstock, p62cr dave stamboulis / Alamy Stock Photo, p62bl Jim DeLillo / iStock, p62br KINGWILL Marilyn/ArenaPAL, p63 "Claire Zachanassian" designed by Susan Hilferty, Friedrich Dürrenmatt's *The Visit*, Goodman Theatre, directed by Frank Galati, p64-65 an extract from *Trojan Women* by Euripides, Edexcel Exam paper: UA007584 Edexcel *Advanced GCSE in Drama & Theatre Studies*, Unit 6, Text 2, p69 aberCPC / Alamy Stock Photo, p70 Chris Ryan / Getty Images, p72 Kichigin / Shutterstock, p72 Andrei Voznesensky, 'First Frost', translated into English by Stanley Kunitz. Originally published in *Antiworlds and the Fifth Ace: Poetry by Andrei Voznesensky*, a bilingual edition, edited by Patricia Blake and Max Hayward (Basic Books, 1966) and collected in *An Arrow in the Wall: Selected Poetry and Prose by Andrei Voznesensky*, edited by William Jay Smith and F.D. Reeve (Henry Holt, 1987.) Translation copyright © 1966, 1987 by Stanley Kunitz. All rights reserved. Used with permission, p75 m.bonotto / Shutterstock, p76 The Art Archive / Alamy Stock Photo, p77 The headline: "More than 100 Afghan schoolchildren admitted to hospital after being sold 'poisoned beans' that would help them 'pass exams'" by Jack Simpson, *The Independent*, 13/04/2015, copyright © *The Independent*, 2015, p80 Chris Pole / Shutterstock, p83 Luigi de Pompeis / Alamy Stock Photo, p87t michaeljung / Shutterstock, p87b SpeedKingz / Shutterstock, p88 Le Pont de L'Europe, 1876, Caillebotte, Gustave (1848-94) / Petit Palais, Geneva, Switzerland / Bridgeman Images, p89 The poem 'Demeter' by Carol Ann Duffy published in *The World's Wife* by Carol Ann Duffy, © Picador. Reproduced with permission of Macmillan, p90 Gilles Paire / Shutterstock, p95 Pete Jones / ArenaPAL, p96 an extract from *A Raisin in the Sun* by Lorraine Hansberry, © Samuel French Ltd, 2010, p96 an extract from *Cyrano de Bergerac* by Edmond Rostand, 1897, p98l Moviestore collection Ltd / Alamy Stock Photo, p98r Simon Dack Archive / Alamy Stock Photo, p100 an extract from *Cyrano de Bergerac* by Edmond Rostand, 1897, p103 Milles Studio / Shutterstock, p103 an extract from *Invisible Friends*, by Alan Ayckbourn, © Faber & Faber, 1991, p104; p107 extracts from *La Bête* by David Hirson, 1991, copyright © Nick Hern Books, 2010, p104 Nigel Norrington / ArenaPAL, p108 Hill Street Studios / Getty Images, pp109–111 an extract from *The Madness of George III* by Alan Bennett © Faber & Faber, 1992, p111 Donald Cooper / REX Shutterstock, p113t Moviestore Collection / REX Shutterstock, p113b Donald Cooper / REX Shutterstock, p116 an extract from *A Raisin in the Sun* by Lorraine Hansberry, © Samuel French Ltd, 2010, p119 ZImages / Alamy Stock Photo, p122 Rowena Chowdrey / ArenaPAL, p124 Elliott Franks / ArenaPAL, pp120–123; p126; p128 extracts from *Humble Boy* by Charlotte Jones, © Faber & Faber, 2001, p130 Elliott Franks / ArenaPAL, p132 Sheila Burnett / ArenaPAL, p134 Print Collector / Contributor / Getty Images, p134-137 an extract from *Strife* by John Galsworthy, 1909, p138 Everett Historical / Shutterstock.

[Note: the sample student responses in the text have been written by the authors]

Contents

Getting the most from the book...........................4

Chapter 1
Drama and theatre 7
1.1 What is drama? 8
1.2 What is theatre?....................................10

Chapter 2
Developing acting skills 13
2.1 Developing a convincing role 14
2.2 Getting physical 18
2.3 Using your voice...................................22
2.4 Developing dialogue................................26
2.5 Using space and levels............................30
2.6 Applying the skills 34

Chapter 3
Staging and design.................................41
3.1 What is design?....................................42
3.2 Exploring sets and stages 46
3.3 Exploring lighting................................52
3.4 Exploring sound 56
3.5 Using props..58
3.6 Using costume and make-up 60
3.7 Applying the skills 64

Chapter 4
Devising..69
4.1 Responding to stimuli.............................70
4.2 Structuring devised work 74
4.3 Effective group work 78
4.4 Communicating meaning 80
4.5 Evaluating and responding........................84
4.6 Applying the skills 88

Chapter 5
Performance 95
5.1 What is repertoire?..............................96
5.2 Interpreting the repertoire......................98
5.3 Exploring monologues 102
5.4 Exploring group scripts 108
5.5 Applying the skills 116

Chapter 6
Extended scripts................................119
6.1 Exploring a longer script.......................120
6.2 Responding to specific aspects
       of the script...................................126
6.3 Writing extended responses......................130
6.4 Applying the skills 134

Index 143

Getting the most from the book

This Student Book is part of a rich and focused set of resources designed to help you fulfil your potential when studying for the Cambridge IGCSE Drama course.

Through a series of six chapters you will:

- develop your performance skills, both as an individual and working in groups
- learn about the roles of actor, director and designer in creating a piece of theatre
- explore how you can communicate ideas and feelings to an audience
- find out about the performance possibilities of plays and other dramatic stimuli
- devise dramatic pieces of your own.

The aim of the book is to be stimulating and enjoyable, whilst at the same time help you build, develop and apply the skills listed above. Each unit does this through a straightforward structure of smaller tasks which end with a chance for you to apply what you have learned in a more challenging way. To help you, there are many useful features such as **clear learning objectives** for each unit, explanations of **key terms,** the opportunity to keep a **reflective log** (a sort of diary) of your thoughts and experiences, **checklists for success** in particular tasks, and **check your progress** statements so you can evaluate how you are doing.

Throughout the book, photos, diagrams and a wide range of stimuli from poems to paintings will help you come up with creative and exciting dramatic ideas. Most importantly, you will read a wide range of scripts from playwrights as diverse as Edmond Rostand, William Shakespeare, Lolita Chakrabati and Alan Bennett... to name just a few, and in some cases attempt to emulate their writing. Some of the language is challenging and may be unfamiliar, but it is important you don't miss out on opportunities to encounter powerful and thought-provoking works.

Finally, at the heart of your study, you will learn all about the skills needed to be a director, stage performer or designer, and how you can make a real impact on an audience.

We hope you enjoy your course – and this book!

Mike Gould

Rebekah Beattie

[Note: the sample student responses in the text have been written by the authors]

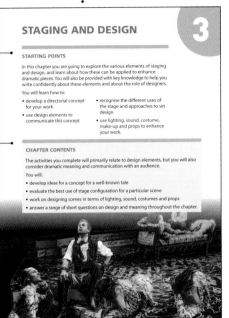

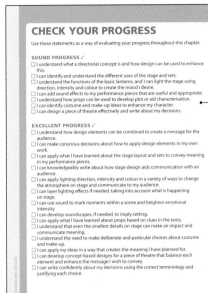

Starting points tell you what you are going to learn throughout the chapter

Opening and closing pages for each chapter introduce and summarise the topics covered

This section shows you what activities you are going to be doing in the chapter

This particular learning objectives are given at the start of each unit

End-of-chapter checklists allow you to evaluate your learning and obtain an overall sense of progress

Key terms are clearly highlighted and explained on the page

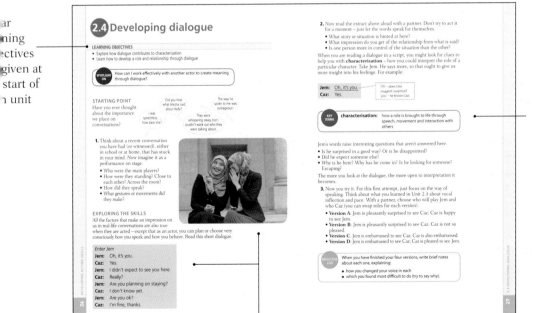

Scripts, photos and diagrams are used throughout to illustrate points and provide visual stimulus

A question at the start of each topic focuses your attention on the key idea or skill to be tackled

For each unit you are asked to carry out tasks and activities, either on your own or in a group

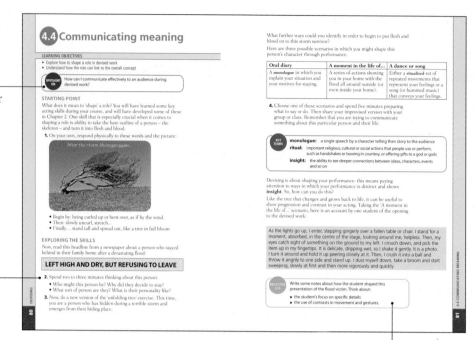

Reflective logs are featured to help you explain your thought processes and record your ideas

Examples of student writing are provided to guide you

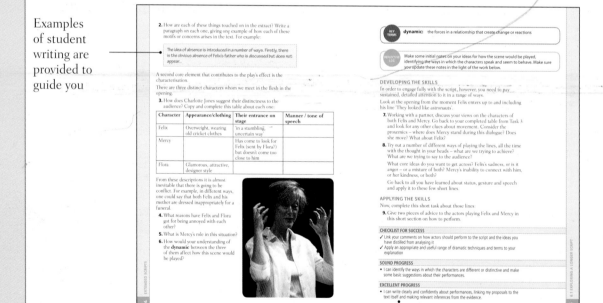

Progress statements and checklists for success are given at the end of each unit so you can evaluate how you are doing

DRAMA AND THEATRE

STARTING POINTS

In this short, introductory chapter, you are going to explore the meaning and interpretations of the terms 'drama' and 'theatre'.

You will learn how to:

- question drama's role and purpose

- distinguish between different ideas about what drama and theatre are for

- reflect on your own motivations and interests in relation to drama study.

CHAPTER CONTENTS

The tasks and activities in this chapter are generally reflective and ask you to consider and weigh up important ideas about drama and theatre.

You will:

- write about people's motivations for taking part in, or watching drama performances

- compare the dramatic ideas of two key figures: Brecht and Aristotle

- discuss the skills and roles required in different types of theatre

- set out what you hope for and expect from studying Cambridge IGCSE Drama in the form of a first 'reflective log' entry

- reflect on the skills you currently possess, and consider particular areas of interest you would like to pursue.

What is drama?

LEARNING OBJECTIVES

- Explore the meaning of the word drama
- Learn about different views on what drama is for

SPOTLIGHT ON What is the purpose of drama?

STARTING POINT

When was the last time you were fascinated by something from real life? Perhaps it was friends sharing a secret or watching a funny video on social media. Perhaps you saw a news clip that made you feel sad or angry. In all of these cases we might say that something happened – a story took place, even if it was a very short and trivial one.

The British theatre director Peter Brook said:

> 'I can take any empty space and call it a bare stage. A man walks across this empty space whilst someone is watching him, and this is all that is needed for an act of theatre to be engaged.'
>
> Peter Brook, from *The Empty Space*

Is this true? This seems a very long way from the bright lights of Broadway, crowds of singers on the Sydney Opera House stage or the elaborate rituals of Japanese theatre. But think about it. Imagine you are the person watching the scene described by Peter Brook.

1. What questions are raised in your mind as the man enters?

EXPLORING THE SKILLS

Drama happens when an audience engages with performers and meaning is communicated. A connection occurs between stage and seats.

Of course, an audience might feel cheated by one person and an empty space. Nowadays, we have certain expectations of drama. Which leads us to ask – what is drama *for*?

2. Why do people write, direct, produce or perform in plays? What is so appealing about it?

   Write a paragraph explaining your thoughts on this.

3. Why do people watch plays, usually (though not always) paying for the privilege?

   Write a further paragraph explaining your thoughts.

DEVELOPING THE SKILLS

Many people have expressed their views on the function of drama. But where does the word 'drama' even come from? In fact, it is from Classical Greek δρᾶμα (*drama*) and means 'action'.

The Greek philosopher Aristotle (384–322 BCE), one of the first people to write about dramatic tragedy, said:

> 'A tragedy is the imitation of an action that is serious and also, as having magnitude, complete in itself; in appropriate and pleasurable language; in a dramatic rather than narrative form; with incidents arousing pity and fear, wherewith to accomplish a **catharsis** of these emotions.'

> **KEY TERMS**
>
> **catharsis:** a build-up of intense emotion that is released in the audience

The 20th-century German writer and director, Bertolt Brecht, had a different view. He believed that if audiences were too swept up in the emotion of what they saw – if they thought it was real – then they could not learn from the drama. Therefore, actors should make it clear that what the audience were watching was a play – a made-up thing. He called this the **alienation** effect, which he believed helped audiences to make critical judgements so they would speak out about injustice.

> **KEY TERMS**
>
> **alienation:** a distancing effect in which audiences are made aware that what they are watching is not real life

4. What does the word action tell us about what is special about drama (compared to, say, a written poem or novel)?

5. What do you think Aristotle meant by saying drama should be an imitation?

6. What did he think powerful tragedies could do? Did he mean they could be helpful for audiences? If so, how?

7. What do you think Brecht thought about Aristotle's view of drama and theatre? Why?

APPLYING THE SKILLS

Both Brecht and Aristotle thought of drama as being very important, albeit for different reasons. They believed it had a social, political and educational function. Perhaps you do not think of it like this. Perhaps for you it is about gaining confidence – or simply having fun.

> **REFLECTIVE LOG**
>
> What do you hope to get from studying for the Cambridge IGCSE Drama course (apart from a qualification)?
>
> Write 75–100 words identifying your hopes and expectations.

SOUND PROGRESS

- I understand that there are different views on what the purpose of drama is.

EXCELLENT PROGRESS

- I can outline my own views and explain whether I agree with Brecht or Aristotle.

What is theatre?

- Identify different interpretations of the meaning of theatre
- Consider your own skills and interests in relation to drama

SPOTLIGHT ON How did theatre start and what does it mean today?

STARTING POINT

In Unit 1.1, you learned about the roots of the word drama and two different viewpoints about its function and purpose. But what about theatre? On the one hand, you probably think about a building in which drama takes place. On the other, theatre can mean all the activities associated with drama – audiences, ticket sales, star performers, performing arts schools, and so on.

But where did the idea of a theatre as an acting space come from?

Like the word drama, theatre comes from Ancient Greek θέατρον (*théatron*), literally 'a place for viewing'. Look at this impression of one of the earliest viewing places in Ancient Greece:

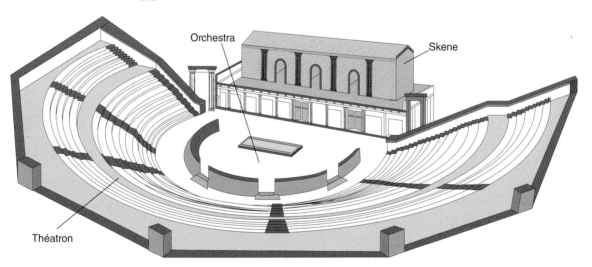

Orchestra

Skene

Théatron

1. What do you notice about some of the words used to describe parts of the theatrical space?

2. How has the use of these words changed today (or what similar words do we use)?

EXPLORING THE SKILLS

Today, theatres share many similarities with those of the Greeks. We still have rising rows of seats, often in a semicircle, and there is an acting area or space, which may or may not be raised. Many theatres now rely on electrical lighting, pre-recorded sound and a wide range of people to manage and put on a performance, whether this is indoors or outside.

Here are some of those people:

- director
- lighting designer
- costume designer
- sound designer
- set designer.

3. What skills do you think are needed for each of these roles? Are they different skills from those of an actor?

4. Can you think of any other jobs in the theatre that haven't been mentioned here (such as **make-up** artist)?

> **KEY TERMS**
>
> **make-up:** the artificial colours and shading added to the face to enhance the actor's appearance on stage

DEVELOPING THE SKILLS

You will explore the wide range of acting and theatrical spaces later in the book, but think for a moment about any theatres you have seen, visited or know about.

5. Choose one of these theatres and write about what it is like:

- Is it an indoor or outdoor space?
- How many people does it seat?
- How and where do the audience sit (if at all)?
- What sorts of play or performance does it show?
- Perhaps there are no theatres: if so, where does any performance or drama take place?

APPLYING THE SKILLS

Think again about yourself and why you want to study for the Cambridge IGCSE Drama qualification.

> **REFLECTIVE LOG**
>
> What particular skills or interests do you have that you can make use of in your IGCSE Drama course? Perhaps acting is your real love, or maybe you are equally interested in other aspects, such as costume or set design? Write 75–100 words identifying those skills and explaining your thoughts.

SOUND PROGRESS

- I can identify the skills and interests I already have.

EXCELLENT PROGRESS

- I can identify the skills and interests I have and can relate these to the Cambridge IGCSE Drama course.

CHECK YOUR PROGRESS

Use these statements as a way of evaluating your progress throughout this chapter.

SOUND PROGRESS ✓

☐ I understand that there are different views on what the purpose of drama is.
☐ I can identify the skills and interests I already have.

EXCELLENT PROGRESS ✓

☐ I can outline my own views and explain whether I agree with Brecht or Aristotle.
☐ I can identify the skills and interests I have and can relate these to the Cambridge IGCSE Drama course.

DEVELOPING ACTING SKILLS

2

STARTING POINTS

In this chapter, you are going to develop a range of fundamental acting skills that you will apply throughout your Cambridge IGCSE Drama course.

You will learn how to:

- develop a convincing role
- use physical acting techniques
- use your voice to create effect and character
- develop dialogue skills when working with others
- use space and levels in your acting.

CHAPTER CONTENTS

The activities you complete will primarily relate to practical work, but you will also be exploring scripts and other sources as part of the process.

You will:

- improvise short pieces based on detailed development of a particular character or individual
- devise challenging physical work with a group work arising from a source text
- prepare a speech from Shakespeare and demonstrate vocal techniques in performing it
- prepare and perform a short dialogue from a modern play
- devise a detailed group work called 'The Interrogation' using space and levels for effect
- answer a range of shorter and longer questions on scripts, processes and performance
- keep a reflective log in which you record what you have done and reflect on, or evaluate, key aspects of your work.

2.1 Developing a convincing role

LEARNING OBJECTIVES

- Identify and explore different techniques for developing character or role
- Apply these techniques to a short, devised task

> **SPOTLIGHT ON**
> How can I perform consistently and confidently in my chosen role?

STARTING POINT

Many actors talk about getting 'under the skin' of a character or role, in order to have **empathy** for the character they are playing, whether a murderer, a madman or a maidservant. But how do you actually do this?

> **KEY TERMS**
>
> **empathy:** the ability to see things from someone else's perspective

Read this extract from an article in which the actor Idris Elba talks about playing the role of Nelson Mandela.

Elba says he constructed 'the feeling' of Mandela from footage from both before and after prison. 'I would literally watch with the sound off,' he says. And he took tips on how older men move from his late father, a shop steward at Ford Dagenham[1]. 'Watching my old man was part of how I made the transition from a young Mandela to an old Mandela. It was about my dad.' But above all Elba says he values the night he spent in a cell in Robben Island[2] (admittedly with an iPad and mobile phone). Mandela's cell was so small that when he lay down on his straw mat he could feel the wall with his feet and his head grazed the concrete on the other side. 'I wanted to understand what it was like to have your freedom taken away,' Elba says. 'I can't compare my one night, obviously, but your sense of appreciation for things is heightened beyond belief.'

Sally Williams, from 'The making of *Mandela: Long walk to freedom*', *The Daily Telegraph*, 7 December 2013

[1] Ford Dagenham: car factory near London
[2] Robben Island: the place where Mandela was imprisoned

1. What two key methods did Elba use to prepare for playing Mandela?

2. Which of these enabled him to be empathetic (up to a point)? How?

DEVELOPING ACTING SKILLS

EXPLORING THE SKILLS

One technique actors sometimes use is called **The System**, based on the teachings of Stanislavski. Actors aim to understand the psychological motives or desires of a character by linking them to their own experiences or emotions. For example, an actor playing a character who suffers a terrible disappointment may try to think of a time when they were disappointed in their own life. They would ask themselves:

- Can I remember the moment? How did I feel? What was I doing?
- What physical effect did it have on me? Did I lose my appetite? Not sleep well? Get irritated with my friends?

> **KEY TERMS**
>
> **The System:** acting technique based on the theories of Konstantin Stanislavski (1863–1938), whereby actors create in themselves the same feelings as the characters they play

Imagine you have been asked to play a character who has just been offered a dream job and returns home to tell their parents. However, the job is on the other side of the world, and their parents are not happy.

3. How would you act this? Identify a time when you were really happy about something you achieved. Imagine the moment and the physical feelings. What was your **body language** like? How did you speak when you told people?

Now, think of a moment when someone told you off, or was cross with you. How did it feel? What effect did it have on your movements and facial expression?

> **KEY TERMS**
>
> **body language:** the ways your body indicates your feelings in posture, gesture, facial expressions

4. Working with a friend, take it in turns to play both roles in this short **dialogue**. Try to actually feel the happiness and disappointment as you perform the lines.

> **KEY TERMS**
>
> **dialogue:** speech between two or more characters

Son/daughter:	So, what do you think? They chose ME out of all those applicants! I can't wait to start life in New York!
Parent says nothing at first. Just crosses his/her arms and turns away.	
Son/daughter:	Well?
Parent:	(*turning round*) You think I'm pleased? Abandoning us to go to the other side of the world. You're so selfish.
Son/daughter:	Oh… I thought… that you'd be happy for me.
Parent:	Well, I'm not.
Leaves room.	

> **REFLECTIVE LOG**
>
> Write brief notes about the short dialogue and preparation. How easy did you find it to recall past feelings? Did it help you in your acting? Why/why not? What do you think of 'The System' as a technique?

DEVELOPING THE SKILLS

There are many other ways of developing a convincing role. Some actors build up a file or box of objects, pictures and music that could be connected to their character – for example, a photo of a sentimental place; an item of clothing; a childhood toy; a pair of glasses; a pebble. This could be done as a collage – all taken from photos or pictures from magazines.

5. What items would you collect or list if you were playing:

- a lonely millionaire
- a downtrodden servant
- a corrupt detective?

Another key way of developing a role is through **hot-seating**. This often takes the form of a sort of interrogation or interview, with you – and other characters or roles played by classmates – sitting on a chair and stool. You ask or answer questions related to the character in the hot-seat.

> **KEY TERMS**
>
> **hot-seating:** taking on a role and stepping outside the drama to answer questions about motives and behaviour

Often it works best if you (and your questioners) have had a chance to prepare in advance. For example, think about these questions:

- Why did I/you do that or behave in that way?
- How did I/you feel when… (something happened in the drama)?
- What would I/you do if…?
- What do I/you think about… (person/situation/idea)?

6. Go back to the dialogue about the job in the Exploring the skills section. Prepare three questions to ask the son/daughter and three questions to ask the parent.

7. Then, working as a class or small group, nominate a person to play each role and ask them your questions (plus any others you can think of).

Preparing in this way can help you to 'centre' yourself. This is the skill of deep concentration, of being 'in the moment' when you perform so that you really inhabit the skin of the person you are playing.

 REFLECTIVE LOG Make brief notes about the hot-seating process. How useful did you find it in terms of building a strong sense of character?

APPLYING THE SKILLS

Go back to the situation with the parent and child. Imagine that the son/daughter is at the airport about to fly off to New York for their dream job. At the last moment, the parent turns up. Why have they come? What are they going to say or do?

8. Work in pairs to think about what might be said, and how each character might behave.

9. Then, decide who will play the son/daughter and who the parent. Spend five minutes thinking about how you feel, and how this will be shown in your speech and actions. Try to bring to mind the thoughts your character might have (for example, memories of the son/daughter as a young child, or as a happy parent after a good exam grade).

10. Now, run the scene. It should only last two to three minutes, but throughout it, try to show empathy both physically and emotionally. Make sure your concentration doesn't lapse.

CHECKLIST FOR SUCCESS

✓ Keep centred on your role and your inner emotions
✓ Think about why you are feeling like this and the effect on your speech and actions
✓ Draw on any of the other work or character information you developed through hot-seating or other tasks

SOUND PROGRESS

• I understand my role/character and can match my behaviour to it.

EXCELLENT PROGRESS

• I can sustain my role both physically and emotionally so that I feel I totally engaged with the character.

2.2 Getting physical

LEARNING OBJECTIVES

- Learn about how to use movements and gesture to create effects
- Apply what you have learned to a short devised piece

SPOTLIGHT ON How can I use my body and movement to make my acting convincing?

STARTING POINT

Look at these two photos:

1. Describe what you see: what body positions and posture do the figures show? How are the figures' hands and arms being used?

2. What emotions or feelings are conveyed? Try not to be influenced by clothing or colour – focus on the body and positioning in each case.

EXPLORING THE SKILLS

Using your body to convey meaning and emotion, or to suggest ideas about character or relationships, is a key skill. One way of practising this skill is to use **frozen tableaux**, rather like the images above. These are body statues you make to represent ideas or emotions.

KEY TERMS **frozen tableau:** a living statue that is created to convey an idea, emotion or part of a story

3. Working with a partner, take turns to mould each other into a statue, as if you were clay. First, try to recreate the two pictures above. Whoever is the statue must allow themselves to be moulded.

18 DEVELOPING ACTING SKILLS

4. Now try out some new ideas. Create statues or frozen tableaux for these emotions or ideas:

Victory   Shock   Sleepy   Memory

Physical drama involves much more than this, of course. In order to use your face and body effectively, you need to break down physical elements into different areas.

How you *stand* or *sit* (posture), for example:

- upright/straight-backed, or rounded-shouldered, stooped, crouched, relaxed
- open (revealing your body) or closed (covering parts of your body).

How you *move around* the stage/acting space, for example:

- pace and rhythm – the speed at which you walk, or enter/exit a scene
- proximity to others – when and why you might move closer towards or further away from someone or something
- profile and position – whether moving or still; what you show to the audience (side view of yourself, back turned, facing).

How you look *facially*, for example:

- mouth and eyes – smiling, narrow, wide-open
- tics or gestures – blinking, twitching, stretching or swivelling.

How you *use gestures* (any movement of the actor's head, shoulder, arm, hand, leg or foot to convey meaning), for example:

- particular gestures typical to a character or role (checking a watch or phone, tapping a foot restlessly)
- gestures to convey relationships (pointing to someone, gently touching their arm).

5. Working with a partner, act out each of these simple situations – without speaking.

- Two neighbours, one angry, the other nonchalant, arguing over a broken window.
- A teacher telling off a bored student.
- A photographer trying to get a photo of a celebrity (who doesn't want to be photographed).

Look through the list above and identify ways in which you could convey feelings/emotions for each one. You are not creating statues this time, so you are allowed to move.

DEVELOPING THE SKILLS

In general, it is a good idea to make your gestures and movements big and slow. Remember, if you are on stage, the audience might be quite a long way away. It is about giving the audience the chance to register what you are doing. You can always speed up later.

Read this opening to a famous novel:

> As Gregor Samsa awoke one morning from uneasy dreams he found himself transformed in his bed into a gigantic insect. He was lying on his hard, as it were armour-plated, back and when he lifted his head a little he could see his domelike brown belly divided into stiff arched segments on top of which the bed quilt could hardly keep in position and was about to slide off completely. His numerous legs, which were pitifully thin compared to the rest of his bulk, waved helplessly before his eyes.
>
> What has happened to me? he thought. It was no dream.
>
> Franz Kafka, from *The Metamorphosis*

6. What has happened to Gregor? How do you think he feels?

The Metamorphosis has been made into a play on numerous occasions, but most productions do not try to turn the actor into a real insect. Instead, they rely on his movements to convey what it is like to be transformed in this way.

7. How would you convey this to an audience? There are some clues in the text you can use to help you. Try miming the opening to the story, using body position, facial expression and gesture to convey the feelings of helplessness and shock.

> **REFLECTIVE LOG**
> Share your mime with a partner or a small group and then think about what you did and saw. Which mimes were particularly effective? Why? How did you feel doing yours? Identify the particular challenges, and how you overcame them.

A common fault amongst amateur actors is that they cannot keep their feet in the same place and they tend to shift about restlessly when they need to be still, either when the focus is on others or when they need to express their own power or personality.

8. Try these two exercises:

a) Decide on a single spot in the room; walk up to it not too slowly, but not too quickly. When you get there, turn and face the centre of the room/space and take up a still pose with your feet planted in one place. Fold your arms and hold the pose for five seconds.

b) Now walk up to someone else in the room. Stop and point out a place on the other side of the room. Concentrate on pointing and keeping your eyes fixed on the spot. Hold for five seconds.

APPLYING THE SKILLS

9. Working in a group of four, you are going to devise a short piece around the opening to *The Metamorphosis*. It will begin with an ordinary morning in the Samsa house. Mother, father and Gregor's sister should come into the kitchen one by one, establishing who they are through their actions and gestures. Then, Mother will leave to go and wake Gregor. She will go into the bedroom to find Gregor transformed. The others will then rush in.

The devised piece will end with a frozen tableau of the family gathered around Gregor. There must be no speech.

CHECKLIST FOR SUCCESS

✓ Discuss, as a group, how each of you will establish who you are
✓ Make sure you use 'stillness' to isolate the rest of the group when Gregor wakes to discover he is an insect (do not carry on acting/moving)
✓ Use the list of gesture/movement skills to create relationships and meaning: who is in charge? Mother or Father? How will this be shown?

SOUND PROGRESS

• I can use gesture and movement to create simple and effective characters or ideas.

EXCELLENT PROGRESS

• I can apply what I have learned about gesture and movement confidently to create convincing characters and establish relationships with other actors.

2.3 Using your voice

LEARNING OBJECTIVES

- Explore different types of voice and vocal effects
- Learn how to use voice and vocal sounds to communicate ideas and feelings

SPOTLIGHT ON How can I use my voice effectively in my own acting?

STARTING POINT

1. Read out this set of short sentences. If you can, learn it by heart so you can say it naturally.

> A: I've got some news. It's important. Are you listening?

2. After you have performed it once, think about the story it conveyed. Did you make some unconscious decisions about A and how he/she spoke? Is the news good or bad? Is the non-speaking character interested?

The words might seem to suggest the news is serious enough for A to want attention, but in fact there are many ways the words might have been spoken.

EXPLORING THE SKILLS

It is important to consider the impact you can have by adjusting your voice. For example, think about:

Pace and tempo	The speed at which you speak and respond
Inflection	How your tone or **pitch** changes according to particular words (for example, 'Really?' could be bored, interested, sleepy, etc.)
Modulation	The volume or intensity of how you speak
Stress	The emphasis you place on particular **syllables**, words or phrases (*'I've* got some news...' as in 'me' not anyone else)
Articulation	The clarity of what you say
Punctuation	Where you pause or remain silent

KEY TERMS

pitch: how high or low your tone of voice is

syllable: a sound part, or collection of linked sounds in a word – for example, 'sunlight' has two syllables: 'sun' and 'light'

3. Try the lines out again in two or three different ways making conscious decisions about some or all of the aspects on page 22.

What impact on meaning does this have? Can it make the lines funny, for example? Or tragic, sad or tense?

Vocal sounds can also add to the meaning. These include sighs, yawns, gasps, laughs, cries, and so on. There are also the speech sounds most of us make – 'umms', 'errs', pursing of the lips, 'tutting', clearing of the throat – as well as the effect of saying nothing, as indicated above.

4. Speak the lines once or twice more. This time, as well as choosing deliberate vocal tones, add at least one vocal sound such as a yawn and a speech effect such as 'umm'. How does doing this affect the meaning or impact?

REFLECTIVE LOG

Write up some brief notes identifying how adjusting your voice and using vocal sounds can change the shape and meaning of a speech, however short.

DEVELOPING THE SKILLS

To develop as an actor, you have to take a real interest in the 'colour', texture and richness (or simplicity) of the words spoken.

5. Words make amazing sounds – say the words below out loud, one word at a time, making sure you **enunciate** each syllable clearly and pausing before you move on to the next.

KEY TERMS

enunciate: speak a word and its parts clearly

infection   chatter   urchin   tumbling   tongue

firebrand

bog   sucks   hiss   pitch   up

6. Were you aware of how the words made you change the position of your tongue or mouth? Were any words more difficult than others? Why?

REFLECTIVE LOG
It can be very useful to develop a vocabulary to describe the sounds of words or lines when you are directing a performance, or explaining delivery. Choose four or five of the words above, and use some of these adjectives (or ones of your own) to describe them: light, heavy, sharp, soft, clear, musical, clipped, flowing, rough, smooth, short, long, deep, dry, round, coarse, harsh.

A key aspect to bear in mind is the attack you give to words.

Enunciating one word is relatively easy, but in a longer speech, your breathing can mean you drop words, or parts of them. It is easy to attack a word such as 'tongue' with the strong initial **consonant** 't', but it is more difficult with a word such as 'infection' where the stress falls on the second syllable 'fec'.

KEY TERMS

consonant: non-vowel letters (every letter in the English alphabet except a, e, i, o, and u)

7. Try speaking aloud the list of words from Task 5 one after the other without pausing too much. Can you keep up the attack, or do some words or sounds drop off?

APPLYING THE SKILLS

In a moment you are going to read from William Shakespeare's play *The Tempest*. Caliban is a wild creature who lives on an island and is controlled by a man with magical powers called Prospero. Caliban resents Prospero's treatment of him as a slave, but fears him too.

8. Read the speech and, applying what you have learned, make notes or annotate it deciding what words or sounds you might stress, where you might pause, any vocal tones or sounds you might introduce, and so on. You might also wish to consider how and where you could use gesture (see Unit 2.2).

Bear in mind that some of the words are **onomatopoeic**, such as 'curse', 'hiss' and 'chatter'.

KEY TERMS

onomatopoeic: where the sound of the word reflects its meaning, like 'chatter'

You should try to use adjectives like the ones in the reflective log task (at the top of this page) to explain how words or sounds might be said. For example:

All[(1)] the infections[(2)] that the sun sucks up…

[(1)] Long, drawn out – stress how much he hates Prospero.
[(2)] Spit out the 'f' in 'infections' to make a harsh sound.

Caliban

All the infections that the sun sucks up
From bogs, fens, flats, on Prosper fall and
make him
By inch-meal a disease! His spirits hear me
And yet I needs must curse. But they'll nor
pinch,
Fright me with urchin-shows[1], pitch me i' the
mire[2],
Nor lead me, like a firebrand, in the dark
Out of my way, unless he bid 'em; but
For every trifle are they set upon me;
Sometime like apes that mow and chatter at me
And after bite me, then like hedgehogs which
Lie tumbling in my barefoot way and mount
Their pricks at my footfall; sometime am I
All wound with adders[3] who with cloven tongues
Do hiss me into madness.

William Shakespeare, from *The Tempest*

[1] urchin-shows: visions of goblins or similar nasty creatures
[2] mire: mud
[3] adder: a poisonous snake, also known as a viper

9. Now try performing the extract. It will help if you can learn it by
heart.

CHECKLIST FOR SUCCESS

✓ Use the sounds and pauses in the speech to aid meaning
✓ Make sure you maintain 'attack' and enunciation
✓ Use gesture, pause/punctuation and vocal sounds to aid your performance
✓ Convey the character and emotions of Caliban that arise from the language

SOUND PROGRESS

• I can speak clearly, adapting sounds to create different meanings for words or phrases.

EXCELLENT PROGRESS

• I can speak clearly, adapting my voice and vocal tones in a wide range of ways to
convey character and create impact.

2.4 Developing dialogue

- Explore how dialogue contributes to characterisation
- Learn how to develop a role and relationship through dialogue

SPOTLIGHT ON How can I work effectively with another actor to create meaning through dialogue?

STARTING POINT

Have you ever thought about the importance we place on conversations?

> Did you hear what Alesha said about Kelly?

> I was speechless… how dare she?

> They were whispering away, but I couldn't work out who they were talking about.

> The way he spoke to me was outrageous!

1. Think about a recent conversation you have had (or witnessed), either in school or at home, that has stuck in your mind. Now imagine it as a performance on stage.

- Who were the main players?
- How were they standing? Close to each other? Across the room?
- How did they speak?
- What gestures or movements did they make?

EXPLORING THE SKILLS

All the factors that make an impression on us in real-life conversations are also true when they are acted – except that as an actor, you can plan or choose very consciously how you speak and how you behave. Read this short dialogue.

> *Enter Jem*
>
> **Jem:** Oh, it's you.
> **Caz:** Yes.
> **Jem:** I didn't expect to see you here.
> **Caz:** Really?
> **Jem:** Are you planning on staying?
> **Caz:** I don't know yet.
> **Jem:** Are you OK?
> **Caz:** I'm fine, thanks.

2. Now read the extract above aloud with a partner. Don't try to act it for a moment – just let the words speak for themselves.

- What story or situation is hinted at here?
- What impression do you get of the relationship from what is said?
- Is one person more in control of the situation than the other?

When you are reading a dialogue in a script, you might look for clues to help you with **characterisation** – how you could interpret the role of a particular character. Take Jem. He says more, so that ought to give us more insight into his feelings. For example:

Jem: Oh, it's you.

Caz: Yes.

> 'Oh' – does this suggest surprise?
> 'you' – he knows Caz.

> **KEY TERMS**
>
> **characterisation:** how a role is brought to life through speech, movement and interaction with others

Jem's words raise interesting questions that aren't answered here.

- Is he surprised in a good way? Or is he disappointed?
- Did he expect someone else?
- Why is he here? Why has he come in? Is he looking for someone? Escaping?

The more you look at the dialogue, the more open to interpretation it becomes.

3. Now you try it. For this first attempt, just focus on the way of speaking. Think about what you learned in Unit 2.3 about vocal inflection and pace. With a partner, choose who will play Jem and who Caz (you can swap roles for each version).

- **Version A**: Jem is pleasantly surprised to see Caz; Caz is happy to see Jem.
- **Version B**: Jem is pleasantly surprised to see Caz; Caz is not so pleased.
- **Version C**: Jem is embarrassed to see Caz; Caz is also embarrassed.
- **Version D**: Jem is embarrassed to see Caz; Caz is pleased to see Jem.

> **REFLECTIVE LOG**
>
> When you have finished your four versions, write brief notes about each one, explaining:
>
> - how you changed your voice in each
> - which you found most difficult to do (try to say why).

DEVELOPING THE SKILLS

Dialogue is all about interaction. This means that it is vital you discuss with your fellow performers how you will play a scene such as this. It is not just about your own role, but about how what you say and do impacts on others. For example, in the Jem/Caz scene, you might agree as performers to 'break in' or overlap lines, so that Caz's responses sound snappy and impatient.

Now, let's look at the physical movement around the dialogue. Try to quickly learn the lines first.

4. Rehearse the scene using some or all of these movements or gestures:

▲ Placing a hand on the shoulder
▲ Reaching out, but not touching
▲ Turning your back
▲ Coming very close to the other performer and getting in their personal space
▲ Sitting down
▲ Standing up
▲ Placing your hand outstretched, palm towards the other performer as if to say 'don't come any closer!'
▲ Using a particular **mannerism**, such as a twitching eye or laughing nervously

KEY TERMS

mannerism: a regular or repeated way of speaking or moving

- Try out several versions, but don't overload the scene with movements. Less is more in this regard.
- Use the technique of 'marking the moment'. One way of doing this is to 'freeze' the scene at a particular line, and explore the effect or relationships at that precise moment. Who is doing what? Where are they looking? How could we adjust this?
- Once you have rehearsed a few times, choose one version and show it to the rest of the class or group.
- What impression was given of the relationship between Caz and Jem? Did everyone present them in a similar way, or were there any surprising differences?

REFLECTIVE LOG

Write about one or two of the performances you watch.

- Can you identify any particular performances that stood out or interpreted the scene differently from the rest?
- What particular gestures or movements were used? How did these affect how you saw the relationship?

APPLYING THE SKILLS

Being able to explore written dialogue, or dialogue in devised work, in a range of ways will help you see the **nuances** of character that make performance interesting.

> **KEY TERMS**
>
> **nuance:** subtle shade of meaning

Read this extract from the opening to the play *Sparkleshark* by Philip Ridley. Polly has gone to the rooftop of her block of flats to fix the satellite dish for her TV. There she discovers Jake, who is writing. Polly starts reading his words.

Jake:	Is it really magical?
Polly:	What?
Jake:	My writing.
Polly:	Bits.

Pause

Jake:	I…I was wondering whose dish that was.

Pause

	I'm Jake.
Polly:	I know.
Jake:	How?
Polly:	Oh, please – Your eyes! Use them!

Indicates her school uniform.

Jake:	You go to my school!
Polly:	Started last week.

Philip Ridley, from *Sparkleshark*

5. Make some quick notes about the two characters and their relationship, based on this dialogue. Who is 'in control' or seems to have more power? Why?

Write three or four key ways this might be shown in the interaction and way of speaking.

6. Working with a partner, develop and perform this short scene.

CHECKLIST FOR SUCCESS

✓ Use the clues, if any, in the script as it stands
✓ Think about vocal tones and pace, as well as how quickly or slowly each character responds
✓ Consider gestures and movements to convey power and emotional state

SOUND PROGRESS

- I can shape and alter the way a dialogue is performed to give a strong sense of character.

EXCELLENT PROGRESS

- I can interpret a dialogue in a range of interesting ways, applying what I know about vocal and physical skills to create meaning.

2.5 Using space and levels

LEARNING OBJECTIVES

- Explore how groups of actors can interact on stage effectively and imaginatively
- Learn how to use space and levels to create meaning and impact

> **SPOTLIGHT ON**
>
> How can I use space and levels effectively when I am acting?

STARTING POINT

Exploring how you use space – **proxemics** – in drama, is fundamental to understanding what happens on stage. Think back to the work you did on the Caz/Jem exercise in Unit 2.4. Whether accidentally, or deliberately, you probably used the space between you and your partner to tell the audience something about the emotions or relationship.

> **KEY TERMS**
>
> **proxemics:** the study of the amount of space between people and how it is used; in drama, this can be between members of the cast, or between the cast and the audience

Look at this famous painting. It is called *And when did you last see your father?* by William Frederick Yeames and represents a moment during the English Civil War in the 17th century.

1. Discuss briefly, with a partner, what you notice about:
   - the *position* of each person in the frame (are they at the side, background or foreground?)
   - the *level* of each person (whether sitting, standing, higher, lower)
   - the *space* around and between some people and others (and what things, if any, are between them)
   - where people are *looking* (direction and focus): who isn't looking at the boy?

EXPLORING THE SKILLS

Identifying how the characters are 'framed' in the painting, and their exact position in relation to each other, is fundamental to our reading of the painting. There is intense focus on the boy, but the large desk between the boy and his interrogator, and the way he is standing on the footstool, emphasises how young he is and adds to our feelings of sympathy.

2. Look at this diagram, which is part of proxemics theory.

   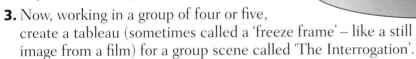

   Working with a partner, try out the phrase, 'How are you feeling?' standing in the three positions shown in the diagram: in each case, the person asking the question moves nearer and nearer.

   Then, discuss with each other how you felt (both as the questioner and the person who stays still) in each position.

3. Now, working in a group of four or five, create a tableau (sometimes called a 'freeze frame' – like a still image from a film) for a group scene called 'The Interrogation'.

   At least one member of your group must be the person being interrogated, but who might the others be? How might they stand or sit – and where? How (if at all) will you use the intimate, personal or social spaces?

4. Share your tableau with the rest of the class, and look at their tableaux.

   How has each group used the space? What can it tell us about the relationships? (Who is in charge, for example?)

5. Now, in your group try similar tableaux for each of the ideas below.

   Take it in turns within your group to be the photographer or director, sculpting the rest of the group into position. In each case, work out how you can use space and the direction people are looking in to create specific focus.

Title 1:	Red carpet movie premiere
Title 2:	Exam results day
Title 3:	The break-up

REFLECTIVE LOG — Write some brief notes identifying what you have learned about space and its effect on meaning.

DEVELOPING THE SKILLS

Different levels can be created in lots of ways within the acting space. For example:

- through characters lying down, sitting, or standing
- through physical stage features such as **rostra** and other parts of the set (ladders, ropes, balconies, trap-doors).

> **KEY TERMS**
>
> **rostrum (pl. rostra):** a platform or raised area of the stage

Such levels can be used in a variety of ways, for example:

- by the actors to convey status, power, or something or someone unattainable
- by the director to allow the audience to see individual characters or to draw attention to particular ones
- by the stage designer to signify different locations or times
- and, more simply, to add interest to a stage set.

6. Think again about your tableaux (Red carpet movie premiere; Exam results day; The break-up). Did you use levels in any way? What could you have added?

Now read this short extract from a play called *Sand Burial*. Children on an island have discovered the remains of an old Viking ship. Sigurd, a ghost from the past, has come to collect the final piece – the steering board.

Raheem and Selima are standing by the rocks when the figure emerges.

Raheem: Sigurd! You came back...

Sigurd says nothing, but stops a few paces from them both.

Sigurd: You spoke of our secret.

Raheem looks uneasy.

Selima: He didn't have a choice.

Raheem: I was trying to protect the steerboard, the final piece of the ship.

Sigurd: (*angry*) I am the guardian. If I do not retrieve it, I will be condemned to ......(*pause, then more softly*) I shall not speak of such things.

Selima: What things?

Sigurd: You think me a big man? A brave man?

Raheem: Yes – you are!

Sigurd looks at the skies. And then around him.

Selima: What is the matter, Sigurd?

Sigurd: They are watching us. Perhaps you are safe. But they will destroy me.

7. In a group of three or four, discuss how you might use levels to:

- draw attention to Sigurd as the main focus of the scene (how would it change the scene if he entered from above or behind Raheem? Or if Raheem were watching Sigurd from on high as he entered the scene?)
- draw attention to a character's actions or emotions (for example, will Sigurd remain standing?)

8. Now, try the scene out (if you are a group of four, one can be the director). If you have access to rostra or other physical levels, use them if you wish. Attempt to be creative and different – it is worth trying out the unusual to see if it will work.

REFLECTIVE LOG Write two paragraphs about how your group used levels in this short extract. What effect did it have on the way the characters were seen? Did it add any new dimension or drama to the extract?

APPLYING THE SKILLS

9. Now, think again about the title, 'The Interrogation'. In the same group, or a slightly larger one if it helps, develop a short devised scene on the title. It should last no more than two to three minutes and should involve a prisoner being brought in. In your group, think carefully about how you could use levels and space to tell the story. For example:

- Does the interrogator have to remain in control? Are there figures of higher authority in the room?
- What about the prisoner? What have they done – and might they turn the tables on the interrogation team?
- Who are the others in the room? Are they guards, reporters – or what? You decide.

10. Rehearse and then show your scene to the rest of the class.

CHECKLIST FOR SUCCESS

✓ Consider the proxemics related to personal, social and intimate space
✓ Think about how different levels of height that characters can adopt can change perceptions
✓ Explore how platforms or simple stage levels can be used for a purpose

SOUND PROGRESS

- I can identify the ways in which space and levels can affect meaning in my drama work.

EXCELLENT PROGRESS

- I understand how proxemics and use of levels contribute to drama in a variety of ways and I can apply these to my own work.

2.6 Applying the skills

- Explore characterisation in a script and the potential for performance
- Apply the skills you have learned about to a character or characters in a script

SPOTLIGHT ON How can I demonstrate my acting skills to their best effect?

STARTING POINT

1. What do you remember about the acting skills you have developed so far? With a partner, take each of these areas in turn and discuss what you have learned, explaining any key terms or ideas you remember.

   Use the image on the right as a memory aid to help you think about some of the key aspects of acting.

You may recall reading a speech by Caliban in Unit 2.3, 'Using your voice'. Caliban is a creature living on a magical island controlled by a powerful Duke. The Duke and his daughter were marooned on the island many years earlier by the Duke's enemies. The Duke, called Prospero, taught Caliban to speak, but Caliban tried to attack his daughter, so Prospero now treats him like a slave.

2. With a partner, take up the exact position shown in the image above. Then bring the scene to life by improvising the conversation between Prospero and Caliban. Use your own words but include as many of these actual lines from the play as you can. Run it for a minute or two.

'Thou poisonous slave'   'A south-west blow on ye and blister you all o'er!'

'Tonight thou shalt have cramps'   'This island's mine'   'I have used thee…with human care'

'I loved thee…'   'Thou most lying slave'   'Vile race'

REFLECTIVE LOG How easy was it for you to draw on the skills you have learned so far? Will you be able to apply this knowledge to written scripts?

EXPLORING THE SKILLS

The work you do on developing your own acting skills will feed into the work you do on the pre-release play script. This book deals with pre-release material in more detail in Chapter 6, 'Extended scripts', but it is good practice to work with a given script as a starting point, both for examination work and for your devised and script-based coursework.

Before you can apply acting skills to a scripted piece, whether as performer or as reader, you need to understand the character and their relationships with others.

Read this information about Ira, a character from a play called *Red Velvet* by Lolita Chakrabarti.

Ira is a black American actor in London in the 1830s. He has just started playing the part of 'Othello', a North African soldier, in a tragedy by Shakespeare, but it is highly unusual for a black actor to get a leading role at this time. If he is successful, he believes he and his wife, Margaret, will be able to settle down. This scene takes place just after a performance – his wife has come to his dressing room.

Now read this extract from the play:

He looks at her with affection and need.

Margaret: I thought… you were very powerful… you stood out enormously. You played… more, erm… more fury than I've seen you play before…

Ira: When?

Margaret: Er… well… it was erm… let me see… towards the end… Act Four…

Ira: It's accumulative. They have to feel the pain of his breakdown…

Margaret: Yes.

Ira: To touch the gallery you have to generate more emotion than sometimes feels possible.

Margaret: I thought you pitched it ever so well… I was devastated by the end. The silence in the theatre was so absolute I didn't dare move. And when everyone stood up – well… I was crying for Othello and… and with pride.

He looks at her and smiles. They embrace.

Margaret: I can't believe we're here. After all these years. It's like a dream.

Ira: A few weeks and we'll be able to rent a proper home. A small house perhaps.

Margaret: Goodness!

Ira: And then we can save to buy.

Margaret: Can you imagine?

Ira: What colour shall we paint the front door?

Margaret: Green? No, blue.

Ira: We'll look back and tell our children, that we…

Margaret: Ira…

Ira: No, we absolutely will… This is the start of a whole new chapter… It's been hard I know. Touring isn't good for family life…

Margaret: Please don't…

Ira: If we settle, it'll happen. You need stability…

Margaret: I have stability.

Ira: I mean a place to really call home. I see how it is, Mags. I'm not blind. Every first night, every public engagement… But you, you hold your head high and sail past, like a swan. For every mean-spirited remark. For all the damp, cheap lodgings.

> Every small, peeling theatre. Every mile you've endured on the road, every penny you've carried to the bank. Every moment of self-doubt you've heard or had. The reason we're here… and I want you to know that I know… I wouldn't be here without you.

Margaret: I don't need to…

Ira: You do.

Margaret: A house? Can you imagine?

Ira: You can stay at home.

Margaret: I can buy furniture.

Ira: You can.

Margaret: Paint the nursery.

Ira: The most important room.

Margaret: It's lovely.

A knock at the door.

Lolita Chakrabarti, from *Red Velvet*

3. In order to try to understand the characters and their relationship, answer these initial questions.

a) Do Ira and Margaret have any children? How do you know?

b) How would you describe the relationship between Ira and his wife based on this extract? What particular lines or phrases suggest this?

c) How would you describe the mood of each of them in this conversation? Does their mood and attitude remain the same throughout?

4. If you were performing the role of either Ira or Margaret, how would you use the script to prepare? Go back to the acting skills you have learned about. For example, can you see opportunities for Ira to move or change position as he speaks?

DEVELOPING THE SKILLS

Clearly, there is a difference in outcomes between acting out a script and writing about how it should be acted, but the skills you need are very similar. In order to explore the acting possibilities, you need to get 'inside' the tone and mood of the piece. For example, look at how one student has annotated the opening lines of a first copy of the script:

> *sense of wonder – it's not quite real. Does she look around the dressing room?*

> *she might pause here, taking it all in?*

I can't believe we're here. After all these years. /
It's like a dream…

> *the sense of the unreal continues – perhaps she shakes her head? Or smiles?*

5. Now do the same for the rest on your own copy, or make notes alongside line numbers.

- Add questions about lines you're not sure of and want to explore further.
- Underline key phrases or lines that need stressing or special treatment.
- Put a forward slash in the script where there might be a pause.
- Add any simple stage directions in note form (for example, 'Moves away' or 'Holds her hand').

Writing concisely about how an actor would play a particular part is quite challenging. Here a student writes about how the role of Margaret might be played, up to Ira's speech.

> I imagine that Margaret is somewhat quieter than her husband, and she is in his domain after all, so perhaps at the start she stands by the door, at the back or side of the stage, slightly cowed, while he takes off his make-up. Her first words should be genuine, but she sounds hesitant, as if she's can't quite explain how his acting made her feel. Her lack of confidence is shown by her 'erm' – as if she is in awe of him. I think she'd be standing still, perhaps nervously fiddling with a hat, or something, while he is big and bold, very animated in his movements.

6. Can you identify where the student has:

- commented on posture and position
- explored voice and tone
- suggested a movement and a gesture?

 REFLECTIVE LOG

Write a paragraph or two in answer to this question in your log:

As an actor playing the role of Ira, how would you deliver the speech starting 'I mean a place to really call home...'?

Use the model answer above to help you.

APPLYING THE SKILLS

You are now going to prepare and perform the script in pairs (or in threes if you wish to use another student as a director).

It is helpful to begin the process by discussing your views about the scene with your acting partner, and agreeing some basic things about the script. For example, here are two students discussing the scene:

A:	I think that Ira is tired – he's just come off stage, but he's exhilarated by his performance…
B:	Yes, but he's even more excited about what the opportunities are – how to improve their lives…
A:	What about her? She seems less convinced…
B:	…at first.

Does this make sense to you? Or would you interpret it differently?

7. Now discuss the script. Decide who will play Ira and who Margaret. Once you have agreed some initial ideas (even if they change as you go on), you can begin to rehearse the scene. For the time being, keep the script to hand and scribble down any notes – for example, about where to stand, or when to move or pause.

8. Learn the lines and perform the scene.

REFLECTIVE LOG Write a full and detailed account of the process of rehearsing the extract, including the decisions you made about acting and why you made them.

CHECKLIST FOR SUCCESS

✓ Use your understanding of the script from your initial reading to inform how you act
✓ Draw on a range of movement, use of space and gesture skills to create meaning
✓ Use your voice in a way that reflects your character and also creates impact on stage

SOUND PROGRESS

• I can make decisions about how a part is played and put those decisions into action.
• I can apply some of the acting skills I have learned.

EXCELLENT PROGRESS

• I can interpret a script in a range of ways, and then develop ways of acting a role that arise out of my understanding of character and relationships.
• I can choose from, and apply, a wide variety of acting skills.

CHECK YOUR PROGRESS

Use these statements as a way of evaluating your progress throughout this chapter.

SOUND PROGRESS ✓

☐ I understand my role/character and can match my behaviour to it.

☐ I can use gesture and movement to create simple and effective characters or ideas.

☐ I can speak clearly, adapting sounds to create different meanings for words or phrases.

☐ I can shape and alter the way a dialogue is performed to give a strong sense of character.

☐ I can identify the way in which space and levels can affect meaning in my drama work.

☐ I can make decisions about how a part is played and put those decisions into action.

☐ I can apply some of the acting skills I have learned.

EXCELLENT PROGRESS ✓

☐ I can sustain my role both physically and emotionally so that I feel I totally engaged with the character.

☐ I can apply what I have learned about gesture and movement confidently to create convincing characters and establish relationships with other actors.

☐ I can speak clearly, adapting my voice and vocal tones in a wide range of ways to convey character and create impact.

☐ I can interpret a dialogue in a range of interesting ways, applying what I know about vocal and physical skills to create meaning.

☐ I understand how proxemics and use of levels contribute to drama in a variety of ways and I can apply these to my own work

☐ I can interpret a script in a range of ways, and then develop approaches to acting a role that arise out of my understanding of character and relationships.

☐ I can choose from, and apply, a wide variety of acting skills.

STAGING AND DESIGN

STARTING POINTS

In this chapter you are going to explore the various elements of staging and design, and learn about how these can be applied to enhance dramatic pieces. You will also be provided with key knowledge to help you write confidently about these elements and about the role of designers.

You will learn how to:

- develop a directorial concept for your work
- use design elements to communicate this concept
- recognise the different uses of the stage and approaches to set design
- use lighting, sound, costume, make-up and props to enhance your work.

CHAPTER CONTENTS

The activities you complete will primarily relate to design elements, but you will also consider dramatic meaning and communication with an audience.

You will:

- develop ideas for a concept for a well-known tale
- evaluate the best use of stage configuration for a particular scene
- work on designing scenes in terms of lighting, sound, costumes and props
- answer a range of short questions on design and meaning throughout the chapter.

3.1 What is design?

LEARNING OBJECTIVES

- Explore the notion of communication, impact and symbolism within design
- Learn how design elements can link together to enhance a director's concept

SPOTLIGHT ON How does design communicate to an audience?

STARTING POINT

In your devising and scripted work, as well as the exploration of an extended extract, you will need to consider the role of a designer and how you would use design elements to contribute to the meaning and intention of your work.

1. Make notes identifying any areas of theatre design that you are aware of or think are particularly important for drama.

EXPLORING THE SKILLS

What impact can design have on an audience? Read the following snippet of a scene from the play *The House of Bernarda Alba* by Federico García Lorca. In this scene, Bernarda has just attended the funeral of her husband with her five daughters. We are told that the mourners 'wear black shawls and skirts and carry black fans'.

PONCIA:	Look at the state of the floor!
BERNARDA:	Looks as if a herd of goats has run over it. *(PONCIA cleans the floor.)* Give me a fan, girl.
ADELA:	Here.

She offers her a round fan decorated with red and green flowers. BERNARDA throws it on the floor.

BERNARDA:	What kind of fan is that to offer a widow? Give me a black one and show some respect to your dead father.
MARTIRIO:	Take mine.
BERNARDA:	What about you?
MARTIRIO:	I don't feel the heat.

2. Visualise this scene and ask yourself:

- What impact is made by the decision to use a red and green fan?
- What message does it give about the character of Adela?

3. Later in the play, Adela comes in wearing a green dress. Ask yourself the same questions again.

These very deliberate design decisions were written into the script by the playwright. Here we have seen examples of prop and costume decisions. Even the smallest details, such as the colour of a fan, can enhance your piece and send a message to the audience, even on a subconscious level.

DEVELOPING THE SKILLS

Theatre design is usually split into four main elements: set, lighting, sound and costume. Each of these can be used to convey a multitude of messages, and they often overlap and complement each other. Design can help set the time period and location of a scene, as well as enhance mood and atmosphere.

A designer will work closely with the director of a play to realise the **directorial concept**. Decisions about each design element will be carefully thought out. For example, a director may choose to set a piece in a certain time period to make the audience think of a contemporary issue, or they might use it to highlight certain themes within the play.

> **KEY TERMS**
>
> **directorial concept:** an approach or overarching idea that a director has for the interpretation of a particular play

An example of how design can be used to enhance a directorial concept is shown in this picture of a set used in a stage version of Charles Dickens's novel *Great Expectations*. In this production, the director wanted to highlight the fact that the story is told through the eyes of the main character, Pip. The director and designer worked together exploring the use of perspective, making parts of the set appear looming and ominous to Pip, who, as a boy at the start of his story, is often beaten and told of his worthlessness.

Look at the picture above once more. This is a Christmas dinner scene in which Pip (the only child character, pictured here bottom left) is being lectured by Pumblechook, the pompous uncle of Pip's brother-in-law. Ask yourself:

4. Why do you think that the table has been designed at a tilt in this manner?

5. What message is suggested by the staggered levels and placing of the adults around the table?

In the same production, another key design aspect was a huge, oversized fireplace in the home of a wealthy, cruel woman called Miss Havisham.

6. What idea or signal might be suggested by the fireplace when Pip, who is very poor, visits the house?

7. Later in the play, Miss Havisham's dress catches fire: what further message might the huge fireplace suggest?

To test out ideas of a concept and ways in which design can develop this, have a look at how one student has identified possibilities around the story of *Little Red Riding Hood*.

Red Riding Hood

We want to make the audience think about the dangers of giving strangers personal details.

We will make this relevant to our audience by trying to highlight the risks that social media presents.

SET	LIGHTING	SOUND	COSTUME	PROPS
Forest – to imply hidden dangers	Low level, cold colours to provide ominous atmosphere	Computer keyboard clicks, 'sent mail' swoosh noises instead of birdsong	Red Riding Hood wears red 'hoodie' 'Wolf' is a man wearing a long black cloak, with a high collar that obscures half his face	Both Red Riding Hood and 'Wolf' have red phones to represent danger Red Riding Hood also carries white flowers to symbolise her innocence

8. What is the directorial concept here?

9. How is it shown through the ideas about set, lighting, sound, costume and props?

APPLYING THE SKILLS

10. Now, with a partner, think of a similar well-known story. It could be a fairy tale or a myth. Make notes on the following:

- What messages are present within the narrative? Is there a moral to the story or perhaps a cautionary tale?
- If you were going to put this tale on as a performance, which of these aspects would you highlight within the piece?
- How will you make the story relevant for your audience? Although the Red Riding Hood example clearly sets the story in the present day, a play does not need to have a modern twist to remain relevant – themes and morals within tales are often enough in themselves.

11. Now complete a similar diagram for your chosen story.

This exercise explores the notion of a concept in its simplest form. This chapter will enable you to look at each design element individually and consider how you can use them to your advantage on a deeper and even more symbolic level. Remember too that sometimes limited resources can be just as useful in promoting creativity. You do not have to have the most elaborate or expensive design in order for your pieces to be effective and inventive.

CHECKLIST FOR SUCCESS

✓ Use design to enhance your interpretations and concepts
✓ Make sure that design elements are conscious decisions, not last-minute thoughts
✓ Maintain a balance of the design elements, allowing them to overlap and complement each other

SOUND PROGRESS

- I understand what a directorial concept is and how design can be used to enhance this.

EXCELLENT PROGRESS

- I understand how design elements can be combined to create a message for the audience.
- I can make conscious decisions about how to apply design elements in my own work.

3.2 Exploring sets and stages

LEARNING OBJECTIVES

- Learn about the varying configurations of stages
- Explore what is important in set design

SPOTLIGHT ON How can I use different stage and set options?

STARTING POINT

1. Think about any plays that you have seen on stage. Were the stages all the same size and shape? Where were you sitting?

When putting on a play, one of the first decisions a director will make is to identify which **stage layout** or **configuration** to use. The style of play, or preferred distance of audience to the stage, are the sorts of factors that are considered.

KEY TERMS

stage layout or **configuration:** the manner in which the performance space is laid out and the audience is located

EXPLORING THE SKILLS

Some theatres are naturally laid out in a certain way, whilst others, such as studios, can be moved around to suit the style or demands of each play. Some of the most commonly used configurations are described here.

End on

Probably considered one of the most traditional layouts, this is where the audience is facing the stage in one direction.

An end on stage gives you the stage map shown here – the areas of the stage universally used by directors and actors to aid blocking. The directions are based on the actor's point of view and derive from times when many stages sloped downwards towards the audience, hence the terms **downstage** and **upstage**. The slope itself is known as the **rake**.

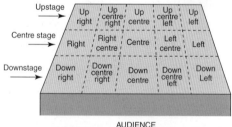

KEY TERMS

downstage: the area at the front of the stage

upstage: the area at the back of the stage

rake: the slope of the stage from the back (upstage) to the front (downstage)

In all your work, written and practical, it is very important to use the correct stage area terminology. This will help your fellow group members and anyone reading your work to visualise any descriptions and ideas that you offer.

2. Following the stage map, what would be the correct terminology to use to describe someone who is:

- nearest the audience exactly in the middle
- in one of the corners of the stage furthest away from the audience?

Proscenium arch

Many old theatres are end on, but also have a proscenium arch, a frame around the front of the stage. Proscenium arch stages were particularly popular during the 19th century with the playwrights of theatrical realism. They helped to create the feeling for the audience that they were looking in on the scene, almost spying on the characters. This imaginary barrier is sometimes called the 'fourth wall'.

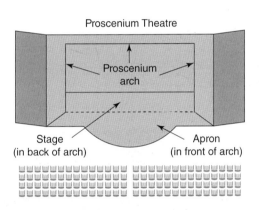

Thrust

A thrust configuration places the audience on three sides. This layout provides a more intimate feel for the audience.

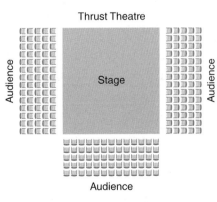

Traverse

A traverse stage is when the audience are on opposite sides of the acting area. It can provide an interesting dynamic for the audience as they can see each other so clearly. It is also useful if there are two different locations in the play as these can be set at either end. Strong focal points are in these areas, rather than centre stage. Often a director will decide which ends are upstage or downstage to make blocking easier.

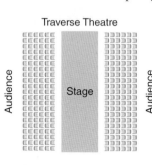

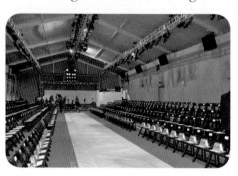

3. How would you feel performing on a thrust stage such as the one pictured on page 47?

4. If you were in the audience around a traverse stage, how would you feel sitting this close if the play were a comedy? What about a tragedy? Would you feel differently, and, if so, why?

In-the-round

In-the-round involves the audience entirely surrounding the stage. It can be used to make the audience feel claustrophobic and is another very 'intimate' configuration. This layout can also provide a sense of fun and audience camaraderie. This configuration does require careful blocking of scenes to ensure that each audience member gets a 'fair' view of the piece.

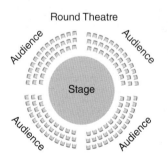

5. What other potential problems can you identify when using a stage such as this one? How might they be overcome?

Promenade

In promenade performances, there is no single, fixed performing space. The audience are required to move around to points where the action is taking place (hence the name, 'promenade' meaning 'walk'.) Promenade performances are popular in large spaces such as warehouses, where the atmosphere of the building adds to the mood of the performance.

REFLECTIVE LOG

Make some brief notes on each of these stage configurations. Which appeals to you the most? Why? Do you think that certain layouts can be used to influence the audience – for example, make them feel intimately close to the action, uncomfortably exposed, or distanced from the stage?

DEVELOPING THE SKILLS

Once a configuration has been decided, the next stage is to think about how the set will be used. Many playwrights are quite specific in their requirements for certain scenes, whereas others leave the design much more open to interpretation and variation. The types of set chosen can therefore be very different:

- Realistic sets try to imitate 'real life' and tend to have details and props that are appropriate to the period in which the play is set. Shapes and sizes tend to be in proportion to those in real life.
- Abstract sets are often sparse and are designed not to imitate reality but to create a 'feel', provoke an emotion or represent a theme. Perspectives (the means of giving depth and height to the set that we see) might be surprising, distorted or out of proportion with reality.

6. Look at the picture on the right of a set used in devised piece based on a true story about a girl who became mentally ill because she was left too long in solitary confinement.

- What sort of set is it? Realistic or abstract? How can you tell?
- What do you think about the colour and use of perspective?
- To what extent do you think that the set helps or hinders the message of the play?
- What genre of play and acting style do you think this piece is?

7. Next, look at the image of a set from *The Mousetrap* and ask yourself the same questions. Is it realistic or abstract? What do you notice about the look of this design compared to the previous one? Why might this set have been 'dressed' with paintings, curtains and cushions?

Both of the sets illustrated serve a purpose for the style of play for which they are designed. With your own performance groups, you can decide whether you want your set to reflect reality or have a more abstract approach.

8. In a group, read through this extract from the first scene from *Amadeus* by Peter Shaffer. The character of Salieri blames himself for Wolfgang Amadeus Mozart's death.

TWO VENTICELLI *are purveyors of fact, rumour and gossip throughout the play. They speak rapidly – in this first appearance extremely rapidly – so that the scene has the air of a fast and dreadful Overture. Sometimes they speak to each other; sometimes to us – but always with the urgency of men who have ever been first with the news.*

VENTICELLO 1:	The whole city is talking.
VENTICELLO 2:	You hear it all over.
VENTICELLO 1:	The cafes.
VENTICELLO 2:	The Opera.
VENTICELLO 1:	The Prater.
VENTICELLO 2:	The gutter…
VENTICELLO 1:	They say he shouts it out all day!
VENTICELLO 2:	I hear he cries it out all night!
VENTICELLO 1:	Stays in his apartments.
VENTICELLO 2:	Never goes out.
VENTICELLO 1:	Not for a year now.
VENTICELLO 2:	Longer. Longer.
VENTICELLO 1:	Must be seventy.
VENTICELLO 2:	Older. Older.
VENTICELLO 1:	Antonio Salieri –
VENTICELLO 2:	The famous musician –
VENTICELLO 1:	Shouting it aloud!
VENTICELLO 2:	Crying it aloud!
VENTICELLO 1:	Impossible.
VENTICELLO 2:	Incredible.
VENTICELLO 1:	I don't believe it!
VENTICELLO 2:	I don't believe it!
WHISPERERS:	SALIERI!
VENTICELLO 1:	I know who *started* the tale!
VENTICELLO 2:	*I* know who started the tale!

Two old men – one thin and dry, one very fat – detach themselves from the crowd at the back, and walk downstage, on either side: Salieri's VALET *and* PASTRY COOK.

VENTICELLO 1 (*indicating him*):	The old man's valet!
VENTICELLO 2 (*indicating him*):	The old man's cook!
VENTICELLO 1:	The valet hears him shouting!
VENTICELLO 2:	The cook hears him crying!

VENTICELLO 1:	What a story!
VENTICELLO 2:	What a scandal!

The VENTICELLI *move quickly upstage, one either side, and each collects a silent informant.* VENTICELLO 1 *walks down eagerly with the* VALET; VENTICELLO 2 *walks down eagerly with the* COOK.

VENTICELLO 1 (*to* VALET):	What does he say, your master?
VENTICELLO 2 (*to* COOK):	What *exactly* does he cry, the Kapellmeister?
VENTICELLO 1:	Alone in his house –
VENTICELLO 2:	All day and all night –
VENTICELLO 1:	What sins does he shout?
VENTICELLO 2:	The old fellow –
VENTICELLO 1:	The recluse –
VENTICELLO 2:	What horrors have you heard?
VENTICELLO 1 and VENTICELLO 2:	Tell us! Tell us! Tell us at once! What does he cry? What does he cry? *What does he cry?*

VALET and COOK *gesture towards* SALIERI

SALIERI (*in a great cry*):	MOZART!!!

Silence

9. Try performing this same section a few times. Each time you work on it, use a different stage layout. Although some of the stage directions imply an end on configuration, do not worry, just try different configurations. Note down how you feel as a performer after each one and what you found interesting or difficult.

10. Ask some of your classmates to be the audience for this experiment and give you feedback. How did they feel with each configuration? Which did they feel worked best and why?

11. What sort of set design do you think would work well for this sequence?

CHECKLIST FOR SUCCESS

✓ Give reasons for your chosen stage layout
✓ Match your configuration to the directorial concept

SOUND PROGRESS

• I can identify and understand the different uses of the stage and sets.

EXCELLENT PROGRESS

• I can apply what I have learned about stage layout and sets to convey meaning in my performance pieces.
• I can write knowledgeably about how stage design aids communication with an audience.

3.3 Exploring lighting

- Learn basic technical terminology for theatre lighting
- Explore the importance of direction, intensity and colour in lighting design

SPOTLIGHT ON How can I use light to enhance my practical work?

STARTING POINT

Lighting is the process of using large lamps to illuminate the stage. It is a key design element and is crucial in creating mood and atmosphere. It is possible to create beautiful and interesting pieces with a minimal set but just with inventive lighting design. Mood, location, time of day are all shown through lighting, and so it becomes a vital tool to consider for your pieces and is essential to write about.

1. Think about how lighting in real life can affect your mood. How do you feel in the following situations:

   - in a changing room that is very brightly lit?
   - outside at sunset?
   - under a stormy sky?
   - on a road at night, lit by street lights?

If light can influence your mood in this way, then it can be used to great effect in your work to communicate to an audience.

EXPLORING THE SKILLS

Next time you go to an indoor theatre, look up. You will see a large number of stage lights **rigged** up pointing towards the stage. These stage lights are called lanterns: these are directed and their beams shaped according to the requirements of each individual show.

KEY TERMS

rigging: the process of hanging and positioning the lanterns on ceiling bars known as the 'grid'

There are many different lanterns, but the three types most commonly used are the par can, Fresnel and profile lanterns.

Par can	Fresnel	Profile
Most basic lantern Focused very easily with 'pan and tilt' movement (up/down and side to side)	*(Pronounced Fruh-nell)* Soft-edged beam which can be adjusted Barn doors (hinged shutters as seen in the picture) can trim the edges of the beam Fresnels are used to light large areas on stage or 'wash' the stage in colour	This lantern provides the most controllable source of light. It has two lenses and the beam can be large or small, hard or soft. Shutters control the spill of light. **Gobos** can be used with profile lanterns

2. Which of these would be best for lighting a very specific small area of the stage?

DEVELOPING THE SKILLS

In order to begin designing with light, there are three main aspects to think about: direction, intensity and colour. By combining these in different ways, you can create a range of effects for your pieces. Many theatres have a large number of lights on at the same time in variations of these three factors, in order to create the desired effects.

Direction

The direction of the beams will allow you to play around with shadows and generate atmosphere. Think of the old trick of using a torch under your chin to tell a spooky story.

If a light is needed to create a particular moment within a scene, such as a spotlight on a character or a **gobo**, this is known as a special.

△ Effects on the stage created with gobos

> **KEY TERMS**
>
> **gobo:** a metal stencil that can be placed in front of a profile lantern to project a shape or image – examples include windows, or leaves to create a forest effect

Intensity

Intensity refers to the brightness of the lantern. It is measured in percentages and known as high and low intensity.

Colour

At the start of Unit 3.1, you explored how important colour can be in theatre design. The colour of the light can create warm or cold atmospheres. Colour filters called gels are placed in front of the lanterns to create coloured beams.

3. In pairs, identify emotions you associate with the following colours. It may help to imagine an empty room, lit with each of them to assess the atmosphere it would create; does the mood feel warm or cold? If you have access to stage lighting, you could do this experiment practically.

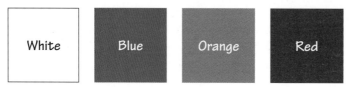

4. What sort of scenes could you use each colour for?

5. Think back to your design idea for your well-known story in Unit 3.1. How would you use lighting to create this piece? Have your ideas changed or evolved?

APPLYING THE SKILLS

6. Look at this extract of stage direction that sets the scene for the opening of *A Streetcar Named Desire* by Tennessee Williams:

> The exterior of a two-story corner building on a street in New Orleans which is named Elysian Fields and runs between the L & N[1] tracks and the river. The section is poor but, unlike corresponding sections in other American cities, it has a raffish charm. The houses are mostly white frame, weathered grey, with rickety outside stairs and galleries and quaintly ornamented gables to the entrances of both. It is first dark[2] of an evening early in May. The sky is a peculiarly tender blue, almost turquoise, which invests the scene with a kind of lyricism and gracefully attenuates[3] the atmosphere of decay. You can almost feel the warm breath of the brown river beyond the river warehouses with their faint redolences[4] of bananas and coffee. A corresponding air is evoked by the music of entertainers at a bar-room around the corner. In this part of New Orleans you are practically always just around the corner, or a few doors down the street, from a tinny piano being played with infatuated fingers. This 'Blue Piano' expresses the spirit of the life which goes on here.
>
> [1] Louisville and Nashville Railroad
> [2] twilight
> [3] lessens, weakens
> [4] odours, smells

In this description, the playwright makes his intended mood for the scene very clear.

7. Go through the passage and make a note of any sections that refer to the mood and atmosphere, rather than specific visual details.

8. Identify and write down clues that will help you to make lighting decisions in the following areas:
   - the mood and atmosphere you want to create
   - the 'temperature' – for example, whether warm or cold
   - time of day and season
   - location – interior or exterior? If exterior, what about windows?
   - Will any specials be needed?

You will not always have so many clues given by a script, but this extract illustrates the sorts of questions you need to ask yourself when working on any play.

9. Make notes on how you intend to use direction, intensity and colour to make your lighting decisions work for this opening scene. Does the lighting change at any point? You may find it useful to complete a table such as the one below for each intended effect.

Intended mood	Direction	Intensity	Colour	Special?

Remember that in your written work, you will have to add a justification for your decisions. For example:

I decided to light the 'wolf' in Little Red Riding Hood from the side to cast long, stretching shadows on stage. This is to represent the darkness and shifting nature of his character and to associate him with the shadows of the dangerous forest.

10. Add justifications to your decisions in the table above.

CHECKLIST FOR SUCCESS

✓ Keep in mind the mood that you want to create with your lighting design
✓ Think about how lighting can be 'layered' to create certain effects
✓ Always justify your decisions
✓ Remember that technology is always changing and there are countless options and developments – for example LEDs, moving lights

SOUND PROGRESS

- I understand the functions of the basic lanterns, and I can light the stage using direction, intensity and colour to create the mood I desire.

EXCELLENT PROGRESS

- I can apply lighting direction, intensity and colour in a variety of ways to change the atmosphere on stage and communicate to my audience.
- I can layer lighting effects if needed, taking into account what is happening on stage.

3.4 Exploring sound

- Consider the various sound effects and how they can add to a performance

SPOTLIGHT ON | How can I use sound to enhance my performance pieces?

STARTING POINT

Sound involves the addition of noises or music played while a scene is happening on stage or during a scene transition. This can be recorded sound played through speakers, or live sounds created either onstage or backstage. As with lighting, sound can be a very useful element in developing mood and atmosphere.

1. Next time you watch a film, identify any sound effects or background music underscoring the scenes. Ask yourself:

   - Does the use of sound in the film guide my emotional response?
   - Would the scene have the same effect on me if those sound effects were not there?

A horror film, for example, often relies on sound to build suspense and make you jump. A comedy may include funny noises to exaggerate comic moments. So too in the theatre, sound is a useful tool to help communicate to an audience.

EXPLORING THE SKILLS

When considering sound, it is important to make sure that it fits in with the style and genre of the piece. Remember that sound in drama is not restricted to recorded effects. If your piece is highly stylised or physical, it may be more effective to use live or vocal sound effects.

2. Write down a few ways in which you might be able to use your voice for sound.

Sound effects can be simple everyday noises such as a door knock, or perhaps more extreme like a gunshot. The need for these sorts of effects are usually written into a script and often played through speakers using a sound desk to control the length and volume levels.

3. What other everyday sounds, such as a doorbell, could you use in your tale from Unit 3.1?

DEVELOPING THE SKILLS

4. Imagine that you have been asked to design the sound for a busy street scene. Step outside for a moment and listen to all the sounds that are around us every day. Write down all the individual sounds that you hear, such as cars, footsteps or birds. Decide which sounds you would use if you needed to create a soundscape (a layered sound picture or story) for your scene.

5. Now imagine that within that scene, two lovers spot each other after a lengthy time apart. How might you 'show' that emotion through sound? It will help to visualise the scene in your head. Consider the following options:

- All sound completely stops until they touch.
- Music suddenly cuts in.
- Music fades in gently as the street sounds fade out (a cross fade).
- The sound simply continues as before.

REFLECTIVE LOG   Write down which of these options you like the best, or if you had another idea, log that. Why did you choose this option?

APPLYING THE SKILLS

6. Look again at the stage directions from *A Streetcar named Desire* in Unit 3.3. The playwright has specified some music, but what other sounds do you think should be used and when? Will your sound design include live or recorded sound effects, or both? Add you decisions to your log.

CHECKLIST FOR SUCCESS

✓ Make sure your use of sound is balanced
✓ Avoid unnecessary effects or music that might be distracting
✓ Justify your use of sound, acknowledging if it is necessary for plot or used to create mood

SOUND PROGRESS

- I can add sound effects to my performance pieces that are useful and appropriate.

EXCELLENT PROGRESS

- I can use sound to mark moments within a scene and heighten emotional intensity.
- I can develop soundscapes, if needed, to imply setting.

Using props

LEARNING OBJECTIVES

- Explore how props are useful for action and characterisation

> **SPOTLIGHT ON**   How can props help me in my practical work?

STARTING POINT

Stage properties ('props' for short) are moveable objects used on stage, which provide two main functions in a play. They can be used to aid characterisation or to help move the action along. Props differ from articles of costume or moving scenery pieces such as curtains, backdrops, platforms or furniture. They tend to be smaller items that a character brings onto the stage and can be easily removed.

Think about the messages that a simple everyday object can convey on stage. What meanings could be intended if a character entered carrying:

- a wet umbrella?
- a teddy bear?
- a pair of ballet shoes?
- a match?

EXPLORING THE SKILLS

Possibly one of the most famous props in theatre history is Yorick's skull from William Shakespeare's *Hamlet*. Hamlet remembers Yorick, a friend, and uses the prop to talk about mortality, and many other things. This scene from *Hamlet* demonstrates the importance and relevance that a prop can have.

Props such as these will be set on stage, but there are also 'personal props', which individual actors should be responsible for. These are items such as pens, glasses, coins or letters, which may be put into a costume pocket or kept on the character's person.

1. Do you have an item that you tend to keep with you most of the time? Perhaps you feel lost without your phone. Maybe as a child you carried a comfort blanket.

Sometimes, as an actor develops his or her character, they like to allocate themselves a prop, feeling that the tangible nature of the object helps with their characterisation.

DEVELOPING THE SKILLS

Read this short extract from the play *The Madness of George III*, by Alan Bennett. The King is ill, although many at court are trying to deny it. Fortnum and Braun are both pages.

> ... FORTNUM, *coming on with a glass chamber pot, runs into* BRAUN.
>
> **FORTNUM:**   Look.
>
> **BRAUN:**   What?
>
> **FORTNUM:**   It's blue.
>
> *He holds the pot up to the light and we see that the urine is dark blue. There is a hint of music which ... should focus the attention.*
>
> **BRAUN:**   I'd call it purple.

2. Does this prop move the plot along or is it character embellishment?

3. Why do you think that the chamber pot is specified as being glass?

4. Can you identify another design element being overlapped here to 'mark the moment'?

APPLYING THE SKILLS

5. Look back over the *Amadeus* extract in Unit 3.2. What props, if any, might you consider using for this extract? Think about:

- the setting and time period of the piece
- whether you would want representative props for the Valet and the Cook, and if so, what these might be
- whether Salieri or the Venticelli would need props.

CHECKLIST FOR SUCCESS

✓ Keep props appropriate: if you're performing a classical script, make sure that your props are of the period

✓ Explore using a characterisation prop, but do not let it dominate or draw disproportionate attention

SOUND PROGRESS

- I understand how props can be used to develop plot or aid characterisation.

EXCELLENT PROGRESS

- I understand that even the smallest details on stage can make an impact and communicate meaning.
- I can apply what I have learned about props based on clues in the texts.

3.6 Using costume and make-up

LEARNING OBJECTIVES

- Think about the signals that costume can give to an audience
- Explore reasons for using stage make-up

SPOTLIGHT ON How can I use costume to embellish my characterisation?

STARTING POINT

Arguably one of the most noticeable design elements, particularly indicative of character, is costume. It can indicate the style, genre and period of a production, as well as giving the audience clues about the characters on stage.

1. Think about how different you feel and look in the clothes you wear to school, as opposed to casual or evening dress. Identify any particular style of clothes that you like to wear that you feel help to project your personality or identity.

2. Write down instances in real life where you feel that people tend to wear a form of costume.

Clothing can often identify us in terms of our social role or by linking us to a certain group. Clothing is also one of the aspects of a person we use to judge them. A designer can play on this human tendency to judge appearance and will often use costume to highlight aspects of character or to contribute to the overall aesthetic and style of a production. Practicality and comfort are also crucial factors to consider. If an actor is performing a very physical role for example, he or she will not want to wear a structured or restricting costume.

EXPLORING THE SKILLS

Costume

When thinking about costume for your pieces, remember how much even the smallest design decision can communicate to an audience.

3. Imagine that a cast is dressed in varying shades of blue, apart from one character who is wearing yellow shorts. What might this signify to an audience? Design details can provide clues and messages about a character.

STAGING AND DESIGN

The painting on the left captures the actress Ellen Terry in the role of Lady Macbeth, a queen from Shakespeare's tragedy, *Macbeth*.

The second picture is from a more recent production of *Macbeth*.

These productions are far apart in time period and style; nevertheless, the character remains the same.

4. In pairs, have a discussion about what these costumes indicate about the character. Consider:

Colour	Texture	Style and period
What do the colour choices suggest to you about Lady Macbeth's character? What might these shades communicate to an audience?	Both costumes appear to be made from luxurious fabrics. Why might this be? Do the accessories add to the effect of the costumes?	The Ellen Terry costume is in a medieval style, true to the time period of the *Macbeth* story (not Shakespeare's time). Do you think that the costume on the right is from a particular time period or of a certain style? If you feel that it is more ambiguous, might the designer have decided to do this deliberately? Why?

DEVELOPING THE SKILLS

Stage make-up

Make-up used in the theatre often depends upon the size of the theatre and the requirements of the individual play. Dancers for example, who perform in large theatres, often use quite heavy make-up. While up close it may look rather strong and unnatural, under the stage lights and at a distance it enhances the natural features.

Many cultures use make-up or masks, or a combination of the two, as a part of very ancient theatrical tradition. These are often used to represent specific stock characters, especially in South East Asian dance drama.

In an intimate theatre, make-up can be fairly minimal and far more natural. Sometimes, however, an actor may need to look older, have facial hair or marks such as scars, bruises or wounds. In this case, special make-up can be used to create these features. This will depend upon character or plot.

5. Thinking back once more to the tale you chose in Unit 3.1, identify what make up you would use for characters in the tale.

APPLYING THE SKILLS

The following character description is from Friedrich Dürrenmatt's *The Visit*. This is the first time we meet Claire Zachanassian, who has returned to her very poor home town as a multi-millionaire. She is intent on inciting the townspeople to kill her ex-lover who jilted her, in exchange for vast sums of money.

> *Enter, Claire Zachanassian. Sixty-three, red hair, pearl necklace, enormous gold bangles, unbelievably got up to kill and yet by the same token a Society Lady with a rare grace, in spite of all the grotesquerie.*

Although you are given some details of her appearance here, the style of her costume is left fairly open to interpretation.

6. How would you costume Claire in order to ensure that her personality was demonstrated, as suggested by the playwright? Think about:

- Colour – What colours would convey aspects of Claire's character?
- Texture – What materials would this character wear?
- Style – Would you modernise her costume or root it in a particular time period? Why?
- Accessories – Would you add any more accessories or props?

7. Do a few costume sketches (an example is pictured on the right) until you are satisfied with your design.

8. What sort of make-up do you think should be used for Claire and why?

REFLECTIVE LOG

Write down your costume choices and justifications for the character of Claire Zachanassian. You could include pictures, sketches or fabric swatches as examples to show your understanding.

CHECKLIST FOR SUCCESS

✓ Ensure that your design choices are always justified
✓ Make sure that you take into account other design elements – for example, costumes can appear different in certain lighting

SOUND PROGRESS

- I can identify costume and make-up ideas to enhance my character.

EXCELLENT PROGRESS

- I understand the need to make deliberate and particular choices about costume and make-up.
- I can apply my ideas in a way that creates the meaning I have planned for.

3.7 Applying the skills

- Explore every element of design for an extract
- Think about how you can express yourself in written answers

> **SPOTLIGHT ON**
> How can I bring all design elements together?

STARTING POINT

All areas of design should be considered when you are developing concepts for devised and scripted work. It is useful to be able to demonstrate and develop your ideas with clear purpose, and to be able to express and justify your designs confidently and concisely on paper. Each design decision you make should back up and complement your overall concept, so that your ideas are made clear to your audience.

EXPLORING THE SKILLS

Read the following section from *Trojan Women* by the Greek playwright Euripides (c. 480–406 BCE). This play is set in the immediate aftermath of the Trojan War and focuses on the deposed Queen of Troy, Hecuba, and her female subjects (the Chorus) who have been rounded up by the Greek army to be enslaved.

> *As dawn breaks, the figure of* HECUBA *is seen.* HECUBA *awakens from sleep and begins to lift herself up.*
>
> **HECUBA:**   Lift. Lift. Lift up your head.
> From Troy's ruined earth, look up.
> We are no longer the Lords of Troy:
> Fortune has flowed against us and
> Crashed down upon our City and our poor lives.
> What remains but misery?
> Country, children, husband: all are lost;
> Family, generations, an entire race – wiped out.
>
> Speak: but what can I say?
> What words will express my woe?
> This hard ground serves as my bed,
> There is no comfort for my aching bones,
> My head and my heart both pound within.
> I yearn to be cradled, to rock to a gentle rhythm,
> To cry unending tears, bemoaning a song of sorrow:
> Music of misery that no one can dance to.

> Come. Come out.
>
> Come you widows and fatherless daughters of Troy:
>
> Join me in lamentation for our dying city.
>
> (*The* CHORUS *begins to enter at this point*)

CHORUS: Hecuba. Our queen. Why do you call?

Why do you call out for us?

We hear your cries. What do they mean?

Have they come for us? Tell us: we are afraid.

HECUBA: My children: the Greeks are preparing their ships.

They are waiting the tide.

CHORUS: But what does this mean?

Will they take us straightaway from Troy?

Away from our homeland across the sea to foreign lands?

HECUBA: I know no more than you, but I fear the worst.

1. Write down your first thoughts about this extract:

- How does it make you feel?
- What is the initial mood of the piece?
- Did you visualise the scene as you read it? If so, write down any instinctive pictures that came to mind.

DEVELOPING THE SKILLS

Do some research about the circumstances surrounding the Trojan War. Can you identify any parallels in today's society that you might want to use for your interpretation? You may decide to set the play very much in its ancient Greek style, or you may wish to modernise it.

 REFLECTIVE LOG Make a research and design log, noting the information that you have found out so far about the Trojan War, jotting down ideas or pasting in pictures that you feel sum up your interpretation. Add to it as you continue with this unit, so that you end up with a mini design portfolio.

2. Now you can think about all areas of design for this piece. Put your initial thoughts for interpretation at the top of your work and refer back to it as you design. Make sure that each element aids and promotes this concept.

Set:

a) Consider the opportunities and limitations your performance space presents. Then, decide your chosen configuration for this piece. Why have you chosen this layout? How did your performance space influence your choice?

What do you hope the audience will gain by setting the stage out in this manner?

b) What choices did you make for your set design?

c) Draw a diagram of your set.

Lighting:

a) What mood will you create? Why? How will you achieve this?

b) Annotate the script with any changes in lighting; for example, how will you open the scene 'as dawn breaks'?

c) How will your chosen lighting affect the colour or texture of your set?

Sound:

a) What choices have you made about sound if you want to use any?

b) If using sound, will it be music, noises, vocal? Recorded or live? Why?

Props:

a) Do you need any props for this scene? (It is perfectly valid to say no, as long as you can explain why.)

b) If using props, what are they and what is the purpose of each one?

Costume/make-up:

a) What time period or location is your piece set in? Is this demonstrated through costume?

b) Is Hecuba dressed differently from the Chorus? If so, how?

c) Are the Chorus members all dressed in the same costume?

d) What colour and texture decisions have you made and why?

e) Do you need to use make-up for any of the characters? What and why?

f) Draw diagrams of your costume decisions.

3. Once you have developed your ideas for each of the design areas, check through again to ensure that they all complement each other and that there is a working balance between them. It might be useful now to think about your school's performance space. Would your designs work in this context? Are there any limitations or extra opportunities that you would need to consider?

4. Read through the scene again. Can you visualise your design? Does it work?

REFLECTIVE LOG In your portfolio, identify what works particularly well and in which areas you have struggled. Would anything need to change to make your design work better? By evaluating your work honestly in this way, you will become a more accomplished dramatist.

APPLYING THE SKILLS

In writing about your designs, you will need to offer clear detail and justification for your design decisions.

Have a look at the examples of student answers to the following question:

> Explain what you would want to convey through the use of stage layout and set in the extract.

Student A

I would set this extract in traverse, as it would make the women feel trapped and the audience feel more involved. At one end there would be a large metal door and the other end would have a boarded up window that the women would try to see through. I would have debris and rubble scattered across the stage to show that the city had been destroyed. The women would be scattered around the stage too, to represent that they are also part of the ruins of Troy.

Student B

I would like to convey the sense of entrapment and helplessness that the women would be feeling in this extract. In order to do this I would set the play in traverse, but with only one exit upstage. This would be a large, bolted metal door to further enhance the prison feel. The reason for this one exit is so that whenever the door is unlocked, all the women can scatter downstage like frightened animals. Downstage, I would have a window that has been roughly boarded up to prevent them fully seeing outside. However, some small cracks would enable them to see out and react during scenes which are happening offstage, such as when Astyanax is thrown off the city walls. By having the audience on either side, I would like them to feel as though they are trapped in with the women, but also that they are partly their jailors. This could make the audience think about situations in the world today in which society's failure to act, can lead to oppression of minority groups.

5. Which of these answers do you think provides the clearest detail and justifications for the chosen design? Why?

6. Now write your own answer to the question, based on your own design.

CHECKLIST FOR SUCCESS

✓ Consider each design element carefully for the effect it creates
✓ Make sure your design elements work together and sustain the style you are aiming for
✓ Justify your design decisions as you progress, so that your rationale keeps you on track

SOUND PROGRESS

• I can design a piece of theatre effectively and write about my decisions.

EXCELLENT PROGRESS

• I can develop concept-based designs for a piece of theatre that balance each element and enhance the message I wish to convey.
• I can write confidently about my decisions using the correct terminology and justifying each choice.

CHECK YOUR PROGRESS

Use these statements as a way of evaluating your progress throughout this chapter.

SOUND PROGRESS ✓

☐ I understand what a directorial concept is and how design can be used to enhance this.

☐ I can identify and understand the different uses of the stage and sets.

☐ I understand the functions of the basic lanterns, and I can light the stage using direction, intensity and colour to create the mood I desire.

☐ I can add sound effects to my performance pieces that are useful and appropriate.

☐ I understand how props can be used to develop plot or aid characterisation.

☐ I can identify costume and make-up ideas to enhance my character.

☐ I can design a piece of theatre effectively and write about my decisions.

EXCELLENT PROGRESS ✓

☐ I understand how design elements can be combined to create a message for the audience.

☐ I can make conscious decisions about how to apply design elements in my own work.

☐ I can apply what I have learned about the stage layout and sets to convey meaning in my performance pieces.

☐ I can knowledgeably write about how stage design aids communication with an audience.

☐ I can apply lighting direction, intensity and colour in a variety of ways to change the atmosphere on stage and communicate to my audience.

☐ I can layer lighting effects if needed, taking into account what is happening on stage.

☐ I can use sound to mark moments within a scene and heighten emotional intensity.

☐ I can develop soundscapes, if needed, to imply setting.

☐ I can apply what I have learned about props based on clues in the texts.

☐ I understand that even the smallest details on stage can make an impact and communicate meaning.

☐ I understand the need to make deliberate and particular choices about costume and make-up.

☐ I can apply my ideas in a way that creates the meaning I have planned for.

☐ I can develop concept-based designs for a piece of theatre that balance each element and enhance the message I wish to convey.

☐ I can write confidently about my decisions using the correct terminology and justifying each choice.

DEVISING

STARTING POINTS

In this chapter, you are going to develop a range of skills related to devised work that you will use throughout your Cambridge IGCSE Drama course.

You will learn how to:

- respond to different stimuli
- structure devised work
- work effectively as part of a group
- communicate meaning and engage an audience
- reflect on and evaluate devised work.

CHAPTER CONTENTS

The activities you complete will primarily relate to devised work, but you will also be exploring a range of acting and writing skills.

You will:

- generate a range of ideas based on a poem called 'First Frost'
- structure devised work based on a news story
- work as a group collaboratively on a given topic/title
- create distinctive roles within a group piece based on an environmental theme
- evaluate a range of responses to devised work in areas such as performance space, narrative structure and directorial concept
- answer a range of shorter and longer questions on stimuli, processes and performance
- keep a reflective log in which you record what you have done and reflect on, or evaluate, key aspects of your work.

4.1 Responding to stimuli

- Learn how to generate fruitful ideas from a range of stimuli
- Consider examples of devised work by other students

SPOTLIGHT ON How can I come up with interesting dramatic ideas from a given stimulus?

STARTING POINT

In your drama work, you will be asked to respond to some stimuli provided in advance; you use the stimuli to devise work with a group, which you then write about in the exam. Here is one form of stimulus: a photo.

1. What story does this photo suggest? Does it show something sad or happy, or both?

2. Who might be the central character? What might have happened?

EXPLORING THE SKILLS

The key skill in devised work is seeing the potential for a story or set of dramatic ideas from the stimulus. This does not have to be a conventional play, but could be a series of more **impressionistic** scenes or tableaux, linked by music, movement or other devices.

KEY TERMS **impressionistic:** providing an impression or idea of something rather than a direct, realistic account

Here are three ideas that groups of students came up with based on the photo:

Idea 1: conventional play based closely on photo	Idea 2: dramatic piece called 'The Exam'	Idea 3: less conventional play but using photo quite loosely
Short play about a student, Jack, who needs certain grades to go to university to study law. He doesn't get them, but his friends do. He has to tell his parents. The truth is, he doesn't want to do law, but is keen on music. The play ends with him pursuing his real love as he leaves home to go busking.	Stylised drama using masks, in which the main character 'X' faces a series of strange tests, exams and interrogations. Everyone in the group except for one student plays multiple roles, including parents, family, examiners, teachers, and so on. Most of the drama is mimed and uses music.	Five characters wait for a train. One by one they tell their stories, each having suffered a recent disappointment. As each person tells their story, the others take on roles from it and show what happened.

3. Which of these ideas do you like most? Why?

4. What particular challenges would you face in each of these? (Think about practical matters such as set and design, learning words, or the structure of the drama.)

5. In a group of between three and six, pick one of these ideas and use it as the basis for a short improvisation lasting no more than four minutes.

 REFLECTIVE LOG How do you feel about devising an unusual or stylised drama? Would it worry you, or would you embrace the challenge? Think about how you might approach this task and write down a few thoughts.

DEVELOPING THE SKILLS

There are two key skills in devising work: the first is in identifying imaginative, fruitful ideas that will interest an audience; the second is being able to structure those ideas so that they create some sort of narrative or logical sequence. You will deal with structuring in the next unit, so for now we will focus on generating ideas.

Here, a group of students are discussing a theme they have been given: 'Bullying'.

A:	Bullying – hmm, well there's lots of that in school, isn't there?
B:	Yeah, so maybe it could be about a new student who's being bullied?
C:	Wait a moment. Bullying takes place everywhere. Does it have to be school?
A:	You mean, like in the park, or at a club?
D:	Or could it be an adult, like at work?
C:	Yes. How about someone who starts a new job, but another worker bullies them...?
A:	That's a great idea!

6. How does the discussion move from the obvious choice to something a bit more interesting?

7. Who identifies the final idea? Is it just one person, or more than one?

The key to good devised work is to allow the ideas to **evolve**. So, a photo suggesting failed exams could lead to work on other sorts of failure, or the idea of exam results could be the start of a drama about something else (the student finding a new friend).

KEY TERMS   **evolve:**   grow and develop in stages

There are lots of ways to get the imagination going. For example, you could:

- take the stimulus (the photo, given theme or whatever) and run a short improvisation, seeing where it takes you and what ideas/stories come to mind
- run a group discussion like the one above (you could do this after the improvisation)
- on your own, generate ideas in the form of a spider diagram, like the example shown here.

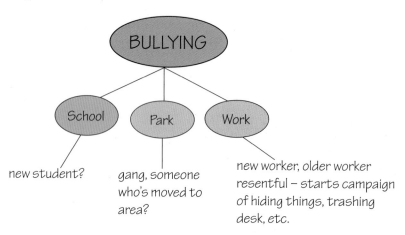

8. Try doing your own spider diagram for this theme: 'Trash'.

9. Then, discuss your ideas with a friend and quickly note down the outline of a story on this theme. The story should have a central character and be in four stages: opening, problem, climax, resolution.

The range of stimuli you may be given is quite wide. You might, for example, be given a poem such as this one:

First Frost

A girl is freezing in a telephone booth,
huddled in her flimsy coat,
her face stained by tears
and smeared by lipstick.

She breathes on her thin little fingers.
Fingers like ice. Glass beads in her ears.

She has to beat her way back alone
Down the icy street.

First frost. A beginning of losses.
The first frost of telephone phrases.

It is the start of winter glittering on her cheek,
the first frost of having been hurt.

Andrei Voznesensky

10. In what obvious ways does the poem already suggest the basis for a drama? Identify:

- the main character
- the scene or place
- the situation (what has happened).

But it also leaves lots of room for you to add information, for example:

- Who, or what, has hurt her?
- What does she do next?

If this were a scene in your drama, where would it come: at the start, in the middle or at the end?

APPLYING THE SKILLS

11. Using the poem as a starting point, come up with at least two ideas for a devised piece suitable for a group of four or five students.

Idea 1: a conventional, short 'realist' play that tells a story.	**Idea 2:** something more stylised and less realistic.
It could be based directly on the poem or might use the ideas in the poem to tell a story about someone else (a boy, for example).	It might involve dance or mime, or the use of masks – it should have more emphasis on physical theatre.

REFLECTIVE LOG

Once you have decided on your ideas, select one for development. Write about how you came up with it and note down key details, such as the main character(s), the structure/story and the style/form of drama.

CHECKLIST FOR SUCCESS

✓ Generate ideas using the techniques you have learned about, such as a spider diagram, discussion or improvisation
✓ Explain the link back to the stimulus and how the idea evolved
✓ Make sure your idea is engaging and interesting, and has a structure

SOUND PROGRESS

- I can identify a few simple ideas based on a given stimulus.

EXCELLENT PROGRESS

- I can generate a variety of ideas and evaluate which is likely to be the most interesting and effective.

4.2 Structuring devised work

- Explore examples of devised work
- Consider ways of crafting and structuring devised pieces

SPOTLIGHT ON How can I contribute effectively to devised work in terms of its organisation and structure?

STARTING POINT

All drama has a beginning, when the action starts, and an end point, when there is silence, the drama closes, and the actors leave the stage or quit the roles they are playing. However, *how* you get to that end point and *what* can be done in the given time will vary widely.

In devised work, you are not constrained by conventional narrative structure, but it can be helpful to consider the dramatic 'arc' of storytelling. For example:

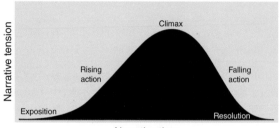

- ▲ Exposition – the opening up, introduction to the situation
- ▲ Rising action – could be a problem or change that pushes the action onwards
- ▲ Climax – the point at which tension and drama is at its height
- ▲ Falling action – could be the outcomes of what has happened at the climax
- ▲ Resolution – the point where the problem, situation or story is brought to an end – happily or unhappily (or both).

1. Look again at the poem 'First Frost' in Unit 4.1. Where might the phone call the girl receives fit in this structure?

   Could it go anywhere? Could it be the end point (resolution) or the starting point (exposition)?

2. Working in a group of between three and six, spend two to three minutes working out a simple sequence for the 'First Frost' story following the arc above.

EXPLORING THE SKILLS

It is useful to keep this general idea of narrative structure in mind regardless of the form of drama your group adopts.

Read this set of notes by one student who has recorded her group's devised work around these four lines of a T S Eliot poem:

> We are the hollow men
> We are the stuffed men
> Leaning together
> Headpiece filled with straw. Alas!

EXPOSITION: a set of scarecrows in a field, still and silent – me, Ginny, Raj and Sam.

RISING ACTION: a small black crow appears (Jimi) – the rest of us (the scarecrows) come to life, break free, dance around, surround the crow...

CLIMAX: a terrible fight – we beat the crow down.

FALLING ACTION: the crow lies dead – we begin to feel pity, tears, sympathy – we pick the crow up, take straw from our bodies and build the crow up.

RESOLUTION: the crow slowly comes back to life – the scarecrows rejoice, but at the sound of the farmer's voice go back to our still positions. The crow runs up to each scarecrow trying to get each one to react, but nothing happens. It circles and then flies off.

3. Would this last 15 minutes? How could you develop this initial structure to make sure it was long enough? Consider the following questions:

- Could you add in an additional scene or two? Could the action move to another location or context?
- Where would speech and dialogue come, and who would speak?
- Are there additional characters you could add (it would mean group members playing additional roles)?
- How could you create or develop the idea of **contrast** in the storyline to ensure it wasn't all on a single level or mood?

4. Try this devised piece out, using the notes above as a starting point. There is no need to stick to what has been suggested, but try to keep the idea of a clear narrative arc that the audience will be able to follow.

KEY TERMS **contrast:** dynamic use of opposites, such as movement/stillness, sound/silence and light/darkness

REFLECTIVE LOG Write up notes on how your group developed and expanded the work from the given poem and student notes.

DEVELOPING THE SKILLS

The structure of your devised work may also be determined by well-known dramatic forms or **genres**. For example, you might use plots derived from *commedia dell'arte*, a type of popular theatre in Italy. A typical scenario would include Pantalone (an old man who represents death and age) trying to prevent the happiness of the Innamorati, the young lovers. Various other characters, including a soldier/captain and serving maids, resist or help.

> **KEY TERMS**
>
> **genre:** a category or type of drama, such as comedy, tragedy or historical drama
>
> **commedia dell'arte:** Italian dramatic style from 16th to 18th centuries with cartoon-like characters, silly plots and slapstick humour

5. You can see here how you might use a typical *commedia* storyline. Copy and complete the table below.

Exposition	Two young lovers meet secretly in the cornfields.
Rising action	They are spotted by a sneaky and jealous plough boy, who reports back to the girl's guardian, a corrupt landowner. Fortunately, the landowner's cleaner overhears the plough boy's meeting with the landowner. The cleaner lets the lovers into the landowner's office where they discover…
Climax	
Falling action	
Resolution	

6. Compare your ideas with the rest of your group and decide on the best storyline. Then run a five-minute polished improvisation. Think about:

- how you can get across the key conventions of *commedia dell'arte*
- how you can make it engaging and appealing to the audience (*commedia dell'arte* is often, but not always, humorous and full of slapstick and physical comedy).

So far, the structures you have considered have tended to be linear – that is, they take place in a single, logical time sequence. However, as long as the narrative arc is present, you can adjust the actual time and events through the use of various structural devices:

- Flashback – at some point in the drama a character remembers or enacts a scene from earlier in the story.
- Dreams or 'flash-forward' – the audience sees future events that may or may not be real.
- Parallel scenes – two or more scenes happen simultaneously, allowing the action to develop in different places.

- Rewind – the whole action takes place 'back to front', either literally, with characters retracing their steps, or by starting at the end of the story, with each scene unfolding through memory or narration.

7. Can you think of other structural innovations you could use?

8. Take each of the structural devices listed above. How could you adapt either the scarecrow scenario or the *commedia* one by using one of these?

9. Discuss these ideas in a group: which ones do you think would be most engaging, original or effective?

APPLYING THE SKILLS

Look at this headline from an international news story:

> **More than 100 Afghan schoolchildren admitted to hospital after being sold 'poisoned beans' that would help them 'pass exams'**
>
> Article by Jack Simpson in *The Independent*, Monday 13 April 2015

10. Working on your own to begin with, identify a potential dramatic storyline based on, or inspired by, this headline. Think about:
- who might be the main or central characters
- whether a particular style or form of drama would suit the story (for example, magic beans are a common element of fairy tales and myths)
- what the narrative arc might be (what the exposition is, rising action, climax and so on).

11. Then, move into your group, share your idea and work together to devise a piece of drama that will last 15 minutes. It will be useful to write out your final devised piece as a script, even if you do not stick to it word for word.

CHECKLIST FOR SUCCESS
✓ Make sure your drama has a narrative sequence and isn't just a series of unconnected scenes
✓ Include a sense of tension or contrast (in mood or movement, for example) that will engage the audience
✓ Ensure you have considered a range of original approaches to telling the story

SOUND PROGRESS
- I can identify a basic narrative structure for a devised piece.

EXCELLENT PROGRESS
- I can consider a range of different narrative structures for a devised piece and help select the most interesting one.

4.3 Effective group work

LEARNING OBJECTIVES

- Explore the most effective ways to work as an individual and as part of a group for devised work

 SPOTLIGHT ON How can I make sure I contribute positively to group work?

STARTING POINT

Your group will consist of students with different characters and abilities. Some may be confident and keen to lead; others may be more reflective and happy to take more of a back seat; still others may say little, but when they do speak, everyone listens.

1. What sort of person are you? Perhaps you are a mix of all of these – after all, we don't behave exactly the same way all the time!

EXPLORING THE SKILLS

Devised work requires you to use different skills at different times.

2. Look at the table below. Give yourself a mark between 1 (low) and 5 (high) for the areas you think you perform best in.

Stages of devised work	Mark
Coming up with ideas (creativity)	
Structuring the drama (vision and strategy)	
Rehearsing and directing (organisation and commitment)	
Performing (confidence and assertiveness)	
Reflecting and evaluating (thoughtfulness and attention to detail)	

This should give you some idea of how you can contribute most effectively to your group's work. Bear in mind, however, that when it comes to performance, you will need to have a role or roles that gives you as much exposure as the rest of the group. This does not mean you have to have the exact same number of lines, for example, but it does mean that it is clear you are a key participant in what is happening 'on stage'.

 REFLECTIVE LOG What is your greatest challenge when working as a member of a group? Make notes on this, and consider how you might improve or change.

DEVELOPING THE SKILLS

The ability to encourage and help ideas evolve is central to devised work. In the 'Developing the skills' section of Unit 4.1, there is an example of how a group helps build ideas, but let's look in more details at what you need to do.

For effective group discussions in devised work:

Skill	Example (what you might say)
Focus: make sure group discussions or rehearsals don't veer too far away from your objective.	'Hang on a minute, everyone, let's get back to our original idea...'
Involvement: make sure everyone in the group contributes.	'What do you think, Carlo?'
Positive reinforcement: when someone has an idea (even if it's not perfect), encourage them.	'That's interesting, Ivana... tell us/show us more...'
Summarising: restate or clarify ideas, when it is helpful to do this.	'So what you're saying is...' 'Ok, let's just stop and see where we are...'

3. Think back to the last group activity or discussion you took part in. Did you or other members of your group work in the ways mentioned above? If not, how would you change the way you work next time?

4. Directing your group's work is a bit like chairing a group discussion: it is your job to keep the group on task and to take the lead on organising. Is this a role that you could do? What would you find easy or challenging about this role?

APPLYING THE SKILLS

5. In your group, talk for five minutes about how you might approach the following stimulus: 'Lost and alone'.

CHECKLIST FOR SUCCESS

✓ Think carefully about what you say to others and how you say it
✓ Keep the objective of the work in focus throughout

SOUND PROGRESS

• I can contribute ideas to group discussions about devised work.

EXCELLENT PROGRESS

• I can contribute positively and help others develop ideas in group discussions about devised work.

4.4 Communicating meaning

- Explore how to shape a role in devised work
- Understand how the role can link to the overall concept

> **SPOTLIGHT ON** How can I communicate effectively to an audience during devised work?

STARTING POINT

What does it mean to 'shape' a role? You will have learned some key acting skills during your course, and will have developed some of these in Chapter 2. One skill that is especially crucial when it comes to shaping a role is ability to take the bare outline of a person – the skeleton – and turn it into flesh and blood.

1. On your own, respond physically to these words and the picture:

'After the storm, life began again...'

- Begin by: being curled up or bent over, as if by the wind.
- Then: slowly uncurl, stretch...
- Finally... stand tall and spread out, like a tree in full bloom

EXPLORING THE SKILLS

Now, read this headline from a newspaper about a person who stayed behind in their family home after a devastating flood:

LEFT HIGH AND DRY, BUT REFUSING TO LEAVE

2. Spend two to three minutes thinking about this person:
- Who might this person be? Why did they decide to stay?
- What sort of person are they? What is their personality like?

3. Now, do a new version of the 'unfolding tree' exercise. This time, you are a person who has hidden during a terrible storm and emerges from their hiding place.

What further ways could you identify in order to begin to put flesh and blood on to this storm survivor?

Here are three possible scenarios in which you might shape this person's character through performance.

Oral diary	A moment in the life of...	A dance or song
A **monologue** in which you explain your situation and your motives for staying.	A series of actions showing you in your home with the flood all around outside (or even inside your home).	Either a **ritualised** set of repeated movements that represent your feelings or a song (or hummed music) that conveys your feelings.

4. Choose one of these scenarios and spend five minutes preparing what to say or do. Then share your improvised version with your group or class. Remember that you are trying to communicate something about this particular person and their life.

> **KEY TERMS**
>
> **monologue:** a single speech by a character telling their story to the audience
>
> **ritual:** important religious, cultural or social actions that people use or perform, such as handshakes or bowing in courtesy, or offering gifts to a god or gods
>
> **insight:** the ability to see deeper connections between ideas, characters, events and so on

Devising is about shaping your performance: this means paying attention to ways in which your performance is distinct and shows **insight**. So, how can you do this?

Like the tree that changes and grows back to life, it can be useful to show progression and contrast in your acting. Taking the 'A moment in the life of...' scenario, here is an account by one student of the opening to the devised work:

> As the lights go up, I enter, stepping gingerly over a fallen table or chair. I stand for a moment, absorbed, in the centre of the stage, looking around me, helpless. Then, my eyes catch sight of something on the ground to my left. I crouch down, and pick the item up in my fingertips. It is delicate, dripping wet, so I shake it gently. It is a photo. I turn it around and hold it up peering closely at it. Then, I crush it into a ball and throw it angrily to one side and stand up. I dust myself down, take a broom and start sweeping, slowly at first and then more vigorously and quickly.

> **REFLECTIVE LOG**
>
> Write some notes about how the student shaped this presentation of the flood victim. Think about:
>
> - the student's focus on specific details
> - the use of contrasts in movement and gestures.

DEVELOPING THE SKILLS

For your role to be successful, it has to fit into the overall concept of your group's devised work. This is what we might call 'integrity'. This means that it fits the purpose of the piece, but at the same time remains distinctive in its own right.

Look again at the devised work on the flood. Here is one group's set of additional characters (not including the person who refuses to leave).

A: A reporter, intrigued by B's refusal to leave their ruined home.	**B:** Another family member who lives a long way away but has offered the survivor a home.
C: An official from the local town who wants the person to leave because it is drawing attention to how little has been done.	**D:** A strange wanderer or outsider who has started visiting B and has befriended them.

Here are some possible overall concepts (big ideas) for the devised drama:

- the individual against faceless bureaucracy and government
- how small humankind is in the face of nature
- how hope can grow from the smallest seed.

> **REFLECTIVE LOG**
> If you could choose, which of these concepts or ideas would you prefer to work with? Why? Are some more positive than others? Could you include all of them in the same piece of drama?

5. Now, look at the list of characters. Develop a 'back story' for them by copying and filling out the character card below. You do not have to use all these details in your devised work, but they will help make your character come to life. Pay particular attention to the motives.

Name (of character, if they have one): _____

Role: _____

Age: _____

Family (if any): _____

Personality: _____

Motive(s) (what they want from the situation): _____

_____

A secret (something no one else knows about them):

_____

6. Now, in order to shape your role further, work with a partner and talk about yourself (the character you have chosen), your life and what you are doing at the flood site. Your partner (and you when it is your turn) does not have to speak, but just nod or say 'uh-huh' – in other words, be a listener.

7. Finally, move into a group and discuss the scenario and the concept you will follow. It could be one of the three listed above or something different (such as a love story or a story of revenge), or it could be a combination of several ideas.

Look at this photo:

8. Is it possible to see from this photo what the big concept is? Identify:

- proxemics and levels
- gestures and movement
- costume and staging.

APPLYING THE SKILLS

9. Prepare and run your own devised piece in your group based on the original headline ('Left high and dry...') and idea. You can use some, all or none of the characters or ideas suggested earlier in the unit.

CHECKLIST FOR SUCCESS

✓ Be clear about your own role and its contribution to the overall concept
✓ Think about how you can shape and develop your role so that it 'comes to life'

SOUND PROGRESS

- I can contribute to devised work by developing my own role.

EXCELLENT PROGRESS

- I can fit my role clearly to the overall concept and 'big idea', and at the same time make it distinctive and individual.

LEARNING OBJECTIVES

- Explore written responses to devised work
- Evaluate your own work in a useful way

 SPOTLIGHT ON   What makes an effective self-evaluation?

STARTING POINT

What are the elements of a successful evaluation of your own devised work? You will need to:

- explain fluently and clearly *what* the overall concept of the work was and *how* you developed the overall concept through aspects of character, space, design, and staging.
- support your explanation with *detailed evidence* of what you did and how the work developed.
- explain what was *effective* and how you or your group achieved this.

Your reflective log should prove helpful here, but the notes you have made will not be sufficient in themselves when explaining your own and your group's work.

Read this response to a short question about the structure of a devised piece.

> Our piece was about how a group of poor villagers discover some valuable ancient coins in the village well. Some of the villagers want to destroy the well to dig up any other treasure that might be there, but others – including my character, the Chief of the village – think there is too much risk and it will lead to a lack of irrigation for the village farmers. This causes conflict and leads to a vote, with the Chief being overthrown. The villagers dig up the well, but there is nothing there. The final scene is of a withered village, with the old Chief slowly burying the coins in the ground again. It was very sad to watch, and everyone understood the difficult choice the villagers had to make. The vote was an important part because the audience play the part of the villagers and they do the vote. We had two endings, but both were sad.

1. What has the student done effectively?

2. What do you think could be improved?

     Think about what you know about dramatic structure and overall concept.

EXPLORING THE SKILLS

3. Now read part of a longer response by a student from the same group, explaining the group's use of space in the devised work:

The performance space we chose to use was a part of the school yard which is shaded by a cypress tree. The dimensions of the space were approximately 10 metres by 8 metres in a broadly oval shape with the limits of the acting space defined by the final audience members' position on either side. We wanted to 'break the fourth wall' so that the audience felt they were part of the drama too – we sat the audience in a three-quarter circle, so that they became part of the village when they voted for whether to dig up the village well. It was meant to be intimate and personal.

> clear identification of location

> dimensions of space

> technical term explained in the next sentence

> how this was achieved

> the overall effect they wanted

We set it outside because we wanted to use the natural light to make it relevant and realistic. The cypress tree was really important because it was a clear entrance/exit point for each character – the idea was that it should look as if each villager almost 'grew' out of the tree so that this stressed the connection between the people and the land.

The focal point of the drama was the centre of the dusty yard in front of the audience. Here, we placed a large wicker basket, which signified the well. It drew everyone's eyes and no one touched it till the final scene when it was slowly taken to pieces, symbolically.

The use of the space, the natural surroundings and the way we created intimacy was effective, but there were some practical issues. Acting outside with bright sunlight and shade from the tree meant that sometimes you couldn't see characters' expressions. If we had thought more about this, we could have used it for Xavier, who played a sneaky villager, but we didn't, so everyone suffered from being caught in the shadows.

4. Now answer these questions:
- Why did the group decide to set the drama outside?
- What was the function of the cypress tree?
- What was in the centre of the acting space until the end of the piece?
- What wasn't effective about the choice of location?

You may not have spent much time thinking about your acting space in your devised work. However, write some brief notes at this point about any of your devised work explaining:

- where it should take place
- what size and shape of space would work for you
- where you think the audience should sit or stand – and in what position – or whether they should move, as in a **promenade performance**
- why you would make these decisions and what the effect of your choices might be.

promenade performance: where the audience members walk about from place to place to follow the drama

DEVELOPING THE SKILLS

It is important that you can explain the directorial concept of your group's devised work. However, as you and your group try out different ideas, your vision (the big idea you are trying to get across to the audience) is likely to change and evolve. Here are one student's notes on the devised work about the village/treasure discussed in this unit:

Week	Structure, action and characters	Big idea / concept	How will it be shown
1	Villagers find valuable items in well – leads to one villager destroying well to get treasure, and leaving village. On the way, he gets lost as he tries to reach big city; he has to sell treasure for water and transport. Ends with nothing.	Moral/mythic story about personal consequences of greed. More stylised than realistic portrayal. Could be any time, any place.	The villager will meet three sets of people on way: each one sells him something for part of the treasure – water, food, a donkey to ride. In the end, he is back at the village but everyone has gone.
2	We've adapted story – Jac had idea to make it more about the village being divided. Now, will be about how villagers vote whether to destroy well for promise of more treasure. Chief is against it, but he is overthrown. Well is destroyed but nothing is found.	Now, we've decided story is about choices forced on a village by climate change / drought – neither choice is a real choice – short-term gain against unlikely long-term survival? More realistic tone/style.	By getting audience to make the vote/choice as if they were villagers, we bring home fact that villagers face impossible situation.

5. What was the original 'big idea' the group had in Week 1?

6. How did the focus of the story change in Week 2 when the group met? What was the new concept / big idea?

7. How did the style of drama that the group was devising change?

It can be useful to try to express your big idea in a simple few sentences or a paragraph so that you have a general feel for what you are trying to achieve.

8. Go back to your own devised work, either work in progress or work that you have completed. What is the overall concept for the work? Write at least one paragraph trying to capture the essence of the piece.

Here are the responses of two students writing about their development of character in their different devised pieces.

Student A:

To play the part of the flood survivor, I watched some videos of flood victims picking through the wreckage of their homes. Some seemed to be going through the motions, not really being able to focus on the reality; others were more practical. I decided to make my character practical, so I decided in the first scene that a gesture was important – she should be mending something, perhaps a torn curtain, or sticking pages together in a book.

Student B:

How does the head of a village act, I wondered? I wanted my Chief to be proud, someone who only speaks when he has to. I thought about wise people I knew – they listen carefully. So I developed this idea that my character should always leave a pause before he answers, to show he is thinking. In the first scene I decided to add a line that would be almost like a catchphrase: 'I am going to look at the stars...'

APPLYING THE SKILLS

9. Make notes on both responses, explaining how effectively each student has explained how they developed their characters.

CHECKLIST FOR SUCCESS
✓ Have they commented on what sort of person they wanted their character to be?
✓ Did they explain how they developed the ideas originally?
✓ Have they evaluated their use of speech or movement?

SOUND PROGRESS
• I can identify and comment on a range of aspects of my group's devised work and say what went well and what didn't.

EXCELLENT PROGRESS
• I can comment on the effectiveness of a range of elements of our devised work, evaluating the ways in which it met the concept we had planned and the effect it had on the audience.

4.6 Applying the skills

- Plan, prepare and perform a devised piece of work
- Respond to tasks evaluating your work

SPOTLIGHT ON How can I plan, perform and evaluate my devised work to the best of my ability?

STARTING POINT

Devised work begins with a stimulus or set of stimuli – this provides the source that will generate ideas that lead to engaging devised work. Whether you are responding to stimuli provided by a teacher, or from another source, the skills are broadly the same. Where you have a choice, it is important to think carefully about which stimulus is likely to generate the most compelling and fruitful work.

Look at the following three stimuli. One is a topic, the second a painting and the third a poem.

Stimulus 1

An unexpected arrival

Stimulus 2

This is a painting by Gustave Caillebotte called *Le Pont de l'Europe*.

Stimulus 3

Demeter

Where I lived – winter and hard earth.
I sat in my cold stone room
choosing tough words, granite, flint,

to break the ice. My broken heart –
I tried that, but it skimmed,
flat, over the frozen lake.

She came from a long, long way,
but I saw her at last, walking,
my daughter, my girl, across the fields,

in bare feet, bringing all spring's flowers
to her mother's house. I swear
the air softened and warmed as she moved,

the blue sky smiling, none too soon,
with the small shy mouth of a new moon.

Carol Ann Duffy

Demeter: in Greek mythology, Demeter was goddess of the harvest. When her daughter, Persephone, was abducted and taken into the underworld, the seasons halted and everything started to die, until Persephone was finally released.

1. To begin with, work on your own and spend 5–10 minutes on each of these stimuli in turn, generating ideas and considering narratives that might arise from them.

   You may find it useful to look again at Units 4.1 and 4.2 to remind yourself of the most effective ways to do this.

2. Note down your ideas and make sure you are able to relate them back to the original stimuli.

3. For your devised work, you will be expected to work in groups of between two and six performers, and your piece should last approximately 15 minutes.

   Move into a group as directed by your teacher. Between you, make a choice about which of the three stimuli you are going to use for your devised work.

4. Now discuss and plan out your basic ideas based on your chosen stimuli.

 REFLECTIVE LOG Make detailed notes on your ideas and the thought-processes whereby your group chose your stimulus – this will be useful later.

EXPLORING THE SKILLS

As already indicated, it is vital you keep detailed notes throughout the process. This can be done in a variety of ways. For example, you could keep a diary that identifies what you did at each stage of the process. Subject to your teacher's approval, you could also take snaps on your mobile phone to use as memory aids. These can be printed out or uploaded to your log and annotated with notes about what you did.

SESSION 1: Group discussion on stimuli. We decided that...

SESSION 2: Trying out ideas. We felt that the stimulus lent
itself to a more stylised way of acting so...

SESSION 3:

SESSION 4:

Another good approach is to focus in on the particular aspects that you may have to write about. One way of keeping track of your work is to create a series of pages for each lesson or session spent on devised work divided into four sections. For example:

Lesson 1: date......................................	
Directorial concept	Characters and structure
Design aspects	Performance space

5. You may not be able to complete all these parts in a single session, but by focusing on them from the start, you will keep them as 'live issues' for later sessions. Copy and complete the tables as many times as you need to.

DEVELOPING THE SKILLS

6. At this point, create a group script for your devised work based on the work completed for Questions 1 to 4. This will need to be as close as possible to what you intend to perform. There are plenty of examples of how to set out scripts in this book (for example in Chapters 2 and 6). Make sure that everyone in your group has an identical script.

7. Then, perform your devised piece with your group.

In a written examination, you are also likely to be asked questions about your piece that will cover both practical and theoretical issues. Look at this exam-style question (written by the authors):

> Select one design aspect (for example, costume, set, masks, lighting, sound) and explain how it contributed to the impact and effect of your devised piece.

8. Begin by checking over your notes to remind yourself of a particular design aspect your group used, how you used it and what its function was.

9. Now, plan an answer based on the following structure, copying and completing the table:

Paragraph	Prompts
1 Introduce the stimulus	*We used the stimulus of…* *We chose this because…*
2 Introduce the design aspect you have identified and your main or first reason for selecting it.	*An important design aspect for us was…* *Our main intention was to…*
3 Explain how it was used and the intended effect	*It was used when/for/to…* *The effect we hoped to create was…* *This was important because…*
4 How effective was it?	*In my opinion, it was effective / not as effective as it could have been because…*
5 What, if anything, would you do differently?	*Having gone through the process, I have learned that….* *So…*

APPLYING THE SKILLS

Here are two further exam-style questions (written by the authors) that ask about your devised piece based on one of the three stimuli given at the start of this unit.

10. Using a structure like the one in the grid in Task 9 on the previous page, write your response to either one of these questions.

> a) What directorial concept did you base your devised piece on, and how effectively did you communicate that concept to an audience?
>
> b) How successfully did you use the performance space in staging your devised piece?

Now look at this extract from a response to Question 10 a):

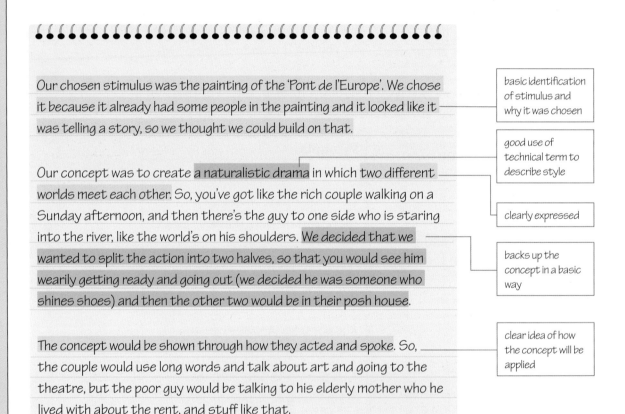

Our chosen stimulus was the painting of the 'Pont de l'Europe'. We chose it because it already had some people in the painting and it looked like it was telling a story, so we thought we could build on that.
— *basic identification of stimulus and why it was chosen*

Our concept was to create a naturalistic drama in which two different worlds meet each other. So, you've got like the rich couple walking on a Sunday afternoon, and then there's the guy to one side who is staring into the river, like the world's on his shoulders.
— *good use of technical term to describe style*
— *clearly expressed*

We decided that we wanted to split the action into two halves, so that you would see him wearily getting ready and going out (we decided he was someone who shines shoes) and then the other two would be in their posh house.
— *backs up the concept in a basic way*

The concept would be shown through how they acted and spoke. So, the couple would use long words and talk about art and going to the theatre, but the poor guy would be talking to his elderly mother who he lived with about the rent, and stuff like that.
— *clear idea of how the concept will be applied*

Comment

This is a good, basic explanation of the concept which identifies what the group wanted to achieve, but it is lacking in detail.

11. How do you think this response could be improved? Look at the 'Excellent progress' pointers at the end of this chapter to focus your ideas.

Now read this extract from a response to the same question:

We decided to use Carol Ann Duffy's poem, 'Demeter' as our stimulus. We felt it played to our strengths as an all-girl group, and we could utilise our dance and movement skills as part of the work.

> explains reason given for choice

The core of the poem is the idea that death and corruption is brought to the earth when Demeter's daughter is taken. According to the myth, Zeus commands Persephone to be released when he sees what is happening to the world, so we created a scene where Demeter pleads with Zeus for his help. This gave us our dramatic arc and climax – would he agree? Myths are like fairy tales with their quests and challenges so this seemed to work well.

> shows understanding of main idea in stimulus

> reference to link between chosen drama and myth

However, because we were dealing with myth, we didn't want a realist style drama but one that was mythic in tone, so we initially adopted masks for all characters. This, however, created some difficulties of expression, so instead we used simple black clothing. A key idea in the poem is the connection between gods and the Earth, so we chose to use our bodies to represent the living, and dying world. When Persephone is dragged off to the underworld, a forest, made from our bodies, withers and collapses. So, a physical, shape-shifting theatre with ritualised speech was the best concept.

> basic comment identifies how style linked to concept

> gives example of how dramatic form can be applied to source text

> sums up concept

12. How is this more effective than the previous response? Is there anything that could have been explained in more detail?

13. Once you have completed your devised work on your chosen stimulus, write a response to the 'directorial concept' task above.

CHECKLIST FOR SUCCESS

✓ Mention your chosen stimuli at the start
✓ Be specific about what you did and the effect it has
✓ Make sure you can clearly link your stimulus to the concept you have agreed on
✓ Provide detailed evidence of how your concept was brought to life
✓ Use appropriate drama terminology to explain your ideas and the effects created

SOUND PROGRESS

• I can identify the basic concept behind devised work and give examples to support my ideas.

EXCELLENT PROGRESS

• I can explain the directorial concept in detail, drawing on specific theatrical forms and styles to convey how effective it was.

CHECK YOUR PROGRESS

Use these statements as a way of evaluating your progress throughout this chapter.

SOUND PROGRESS ✓

☐ I can identify a few simple ideas based on a given stimulus.

☐ I can identify a basic narrative structure for a devised piece.

☐ I can contribute ideas to group discussions about devised work.

☐ I can contribute to devised work by developing my own role.

☐ I can identify and comment on a range of aspects in my group's devised work and say what went well and what didn't.

☐ I can identify the basic concept behind devised work and give examples to support my ideas.

EXCELLENT PROGRESS ✓

☐ I can generate a variety of ideas and evaluate which is likely to be the most interesting and effective.

☐ I can consider a range of different narrative structures for a devised piece and help select the most interesting one.

☐ I can contribute positively and help others develop ideas in group discussions about devised work.

☐ I can fit my role clearly to the overall concept and 'big idea', and at the same time make it distinctive and individual.

☐ I can comment on the effectiveness of a range of elements of our devised work, evaluating the ways in which it met the concept we had planned and the effect it had on the audience.

☐ I can explain the directorial concept in detail, drawing on specific theatrical forms and styles to convey how effective it was.

PERFORMANCE

STARTING POINTS

In this chapter you will develop particular performance skills related to monologues and longer group scripts, and consider different styles and ways of interpreting them.

You will learn how to:

- identify the possibilities of different forms of repertoire
- explore the idea of interpretation and apply this to a script
- explore, develop and perform a monologue of your choice
- explore, develop and perform a group script
- apply the range of skills learned from both formats to a final monologue.

CHAPTER CONTENTS

The activities you complete will primarily relate to performance work, but you will also be annotating scripts and responding to other sources as part of the process.

You will:

- read three short extracts and infer styles and forms of repertoire from them
- explore different interpretations of a famous scene from Shakespeare's *Romeo and Juliet*
- make your own interpretation of a role from *Cyrano de Bergerac* by Edmond Rostand
- develop, structure and perform a monologue from either *Invisible Friends* by Alan Ayckbourn or *La Bête* by David Hirson
- develop, structure and perform a longer group script from *The Madness of George III* by Alan Bennett
- apply all the skills you have learned to a monologue from Lorraine Hansberry's *A Raisin in the Sun*
- answer a range of shorter and longer questions on scripts, processes and performance
- keep a reflective log in which you record what you have done, and reflect on, or evaluate, key aspects of your work.

5.1 What is repertoire?

LEARNING OBJECTIVES

- Explore what repertoire is

> **SPOTLIGHT ON** What is repertoire and how can I extend my knowledge of different types of repertoire?

STARTING POINT

Not all drama begins on the written page. Famously, playwright and film director Mike Leigh works with his actors to construct a script around key plots and characters, using improvisation before the final drama is 'set in stone' and a script created. However, many plays do begin as written works, with writers constructing carefully thought-out action, characterisation, staging, and so on. The wide range of written plays, from short one-act monologues to multi-character epics, can be called 'repertoire'.

EXPLORING THE SKILLS

In order to be able to interpret and work with written drama, you need to have a good knowledge of the range of written drama that exists. You also need to be able to identify different forms and styles of drama.

1. Read these three very short extracts from different scripts. What can you deduce or infer about them from the small amount of information given?

Extract A

> **WALTER:** *(at the window)* Just look at 'em down there... Running and racing to work...
>
> *He turns and faces his wife and watches her a moment at the stove, and then, suddenly –*
> You look young this morning, baby.
>
> **RUTH:** *(indifferently)* Yeah?
>
> **WALTER:** Just for a second – stirring them eggs. It's gone now – just for a second it was – you looked real young again. (*Then drily.*) It's gone now – you look like yourself again.
>
> **RUTH:** Man, if you don't shut up and leave me alone.
>
> Lorraine Hansberry, from *A Raisin in the Sun*

Extract B

> **CYRANO:** ...I ask you only this – when the great cold
> Gathers around my bones, that you may give
> A double meaning to your widow's weeds[1] And the tears you let fall for him may be
> For a little – my tears.
> **ROXANE:** *(Sobbing)* Oh my love!...
>
> Edmond Rostand, from *Cyrano de Bergerac*

[1] widow's weeds: mourning clothes

Extract C

SANJAY:

Not much of a place is it? But then beggars can't be choosers... which is kind of funny, as I was a beggar before they let me have this place. My own place. Well, not mine, strictly – I rent it, of course, but it's better than under the bridge by the river, with the rats, the low-life, the police, the constant cold and... *(pauses)* Best not to think of it, eh? Cos that's all behind me.

Picks up kettle and fills it.

Cup of tea when I want it. My own bed. With a mattress. OK, it's seen better days, but it's a start, a beginning of... well, not exactly a *new* life, but a very good second-hand one.

Mike Gould

2. Copy and complete this table.

Extract	Style or genre	Time (e.g. modern) and mood	Action/characters
A		Modern, realistic, family setting? Informal language	
B			Two lovers, one dying
C	Monologue		

DEVELOPING THE SKILLS

3. What other scripts have you come across in your work from this book, or in class? Can you add the plays to your copy of the table, summing up their styles/genres, time, mood and action?

APPLYING THE SKILLS

4. How widely read are you when it comes to a range of plays in different styles and forms? Look at the list below. Have you heard of any of these forms?

- Victorian melodrama
- Comedy of the absurd
- Revenge drama
- Classical tragedy

Do some brief research about each genre and make simple notes about key conventions of each. Make a list of well-known authors associated with them and any famous play titles.

CHECKLIST FOR SUCCESS
✓ Note down key differences and similarities between styles and forms

SOUND PROGRESS
- I can identify differences between styles of written play.

EXCELLENT PROGRESS
- I can infer detailed ideas about styles, action and tone from a range of plays.

5.2 Interpreting the repertoire

- Explore the idea of interpretation
- Apply what you have learned to a short script

SPOTLIGHT ON   What is interpretation and why does it matter?

STARTING POINT

Think about the moment you pick up a playscript for the first time. What are the questions going through your head? Perhaps you are wondering what sort of person you are going to play? Or maybe you're interested in the action – what happens, what type of drama will it be? Whatever you ultimately decide, your decisions will be an **interpretation**, your 'take' on the script.

KEY TERMS   **interpretation:**   the particular approach taken to a text in order to bring it to life on the stage

EXPLORING THE SKILLS

1. Look at the following images. They are both taken from the same well-known scene from *Romeo and Juliet*. In what ways are they different? Who decided to stage/play them this way?

2. Can you infer anything particular about how the director or actors wanted the audience to 'see' the play from the images here?

The particular interpretation, whether it is a traditional, period version, or something more modern and closer to our own lives, has to be realised – that is, brought to life from the same words on the page that millions of people have read. So, how is this done?

DEVELOPING THE SKILLS

It is a good idea to begin with the script itself and work from there. All the interpretations of *Romeo and Juliet* will have been the result of someone – or more likely, a team of people – seeing something in the play that they want to stress or focus on. However, you need to ask key questions of the script first.

Key questions	What does it mean?
What is the style or genre of the play?	Does the play belong to a recognisable type? For example, is it a tragedy, and if so, does it conform to what we expect from tragedies? (For example, a great person brought down by a fatal weakness.) Perhaps the play breaks with tradition and does things slightly differently – if so how? The style or genre might also be related to a particular movement or time – for example, Victorian melodrama, or mid-20th century absurdist works.
What do I know about the character or role I am playing or working with?	What is my character's role or function in the play? The author may have given me information about them: what is it? Do they wear particular clothes or behave in particular ways? Are they the protagonist or the antagonist, or do they have some other part to play? What effect do they have on the action – does it change as a result of what they say and do?
What are the key issues when moving from page to stage?	How much information has the playwright provided, and how far should I/we divert from this? What are the technical or practical issues around staging or performing? What are the possibilities – how far can, or should, we go?

3. Look at the opening lines, including the dialogue and stage directions, of any play and make brief notes on:

- what the writer tells us about the style, characters and setting
- what is left to our own interpretation.

In order to test these out, you are going to look at an extract from the play *Cyrano de Bergerac* set in 1640. It concerns a flamboyant, witty knight who is both brave and intelligent. He falls for a beautiful woman, Roxane, but because of what he believes is his ugliness (he has a very large nose), does not reveal his love until the end of the play. In the final act, set in late autumn, Cyrano is dying and hallucinating from a wound given him by one of his enemies. He has gone to see Roxane in the park of a convent where she has been living since the death of her young lover, Christian. Cyrano has half-collapsed into a chair by a tree in the garden:

The chapel bell is ringing. Along the avenue of trees above the stairway, the nuns pass in procession to their prayers.

CYRANO: They are going to pray now; there is the bell.

ROXANE: *(Raises herself and calls to them)*
Sister! – Sister! –

CYRANO: *(Holding on to her hand)*
No, – do not go away –
I may not still be here when you return...

The nuns have gone into the chapel. The organ begins to play.
A little harmony is all I need –
Listen.

ROXANE: You shall not die! I love you! –

CYRANO: No –
That is not in the story! You remember
When Beauty said 'I love you' to the Beast
That was a fairy prince, his ugliness
Changed and dissolved, like magic... But you see
I am still the same.

ROXANE: And I – I have done
This to you! All my fault – mine!

CYRANO: You? Why no,
On the contrary! I had never known
Womanhood and sweetness but for you.

Edmond Rostand, from *Cyrano de Bergerac*

4. Based on what you have read, what do you think is the style or genre of the play? (You read a short extract from *Cyrano* in Unit 5.1, so you can refer to that, too, if you wish.) What clues are there in what happens and in the subject matter?

5. What role do you think Cyrano plays in the action? Does he fit in with a particular type of character you have seen in other plays? What clues are we given about his character from how he speaks and behaves?

6. Based just on what you have read here, what particular challenges would you face in moving this from page to stage? You could think about the style of the play, but also things such as costume, design, lighting and sound.

Now, read this discussion between a trio of students considering how to bring the extract to the stage. How effective do you think their ideas are?

Saj:	So, this clearly has aspects of fairy tale. I mean, Cyrano even talks about 'Beauty and the Beast' so I think it makes sense to try to design it in a magical way – like the garden is itself magical.
Tim:	But Cyrano says it isn't like the story – because when she says she loves him, he doesn't turn into a prince.
Emma:	I agree. I think if we play it too much like a fairy tale, it will become melodramatic. I think it needs to be sad and sweet, gentle...

7. What is good about this discussion?

8. Does it go far enough in helping with the design or acting?

9. Now, look at one student's notes on playing Cyrano. How has he taken the script (or the information you have been told about the final act) and 'brought it to life'?

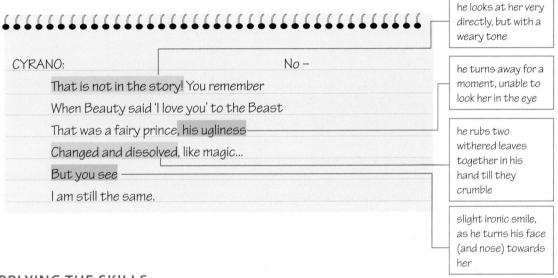

CYRANO: No –
    That is not in the story! You remember — *he looks at her very directly, but with a weary tone*
    When Beauty said 'I love you' to the Beast
    That was a fairy prince, his ugliness — *he turns away for a moment, unable to look her in the eye*
    Changed and dissolved, like magic... — *he rubs two withered leaves together in his hand till they crumble*
    But you see —
    I am still the same. — *slight ironic smile, as he turns his face (and nose) towards her*

APPLYING THE SKILLS

10. Now select either the character of Cyrano or Roxane and, using a copy of the extract, make your own notes on how you would interpret the particular role. (You may feel you need to find out a little bit more about the play/story first.)

CHECKLIST FOR SUCCESS

✓ Bear in mind your own interpretation of the scene – decide how 'real' you wish it to be (in terms of matching the period) and what tone/mood you wish to convey
✓ Consider what particular tones, gestures and proxemics you would use

SOUND PROGRESS

• I can draw my own conclusions about the style of a play and imagine it on stage.

EXCELLENT PROGRESS

• I can infer ideas about a play's genre and style, consider a number of options and use this to make my own interpretation.

5.3 Exploring monologues

LEARNING OBJECTIVES

- Consider factors to help you to choose a monologue
- Explore how to develop a character
- Begin structuring a monologue performance

SPOTLIGHT ON How can I begin to approach my monologue preparation?

STARTING POINT

As part of your work you will be required to choose, rehearse and perform a **monologue** of between three and five minutes in length from any play. This may seem daunting, but you can narrow down your choice by asking yourself:

- Would I prefer a comedy or a tragedy, or something in between?
- What style would I prefer? For example, physical, naturalistic, classical, contemporary?
- When I read the first few lines of a monologue aloud, do I like it? Does it capture my interest?

There are a number of monologue books available, but these will only give you a brief outline of the play and the character. It is important for you to read the whole play that your monologue is from, in order to gain knowledge of your character's emotional journey and objective for the speech. The historical or social context of the play will also give you a perspective on the character and provide you with clues and ideas as to how to play the role.

KEY TERMS

monologue: a longer section of speech that is part of the action delivered by one actor, either alone or usually with other characters on stage

EXPLORING THE SKILLS

1. Read the following contrasting monologues:

Monologue A

In this monologue, Lucy 'revives' her imaginary friend as she feels ignored by her family. 'Grisly Gary' is her brother.

LUCY: You may have heard my mum talking about my invisible friend. Do you remember? Well, that's my invisible friend, Zara. *(introducing her)* This is Zara. I want you to meet Zara. Zara, say hello. That's it. Will you say hello to Zara, my invisible friend? I invented Zara – oh, years ago – when I was seven or eight. Just for fun. I think I was ill at that time and wasn't allowed to play with any of my real friends, so I made

up Zara. She's my special friend that no one can see except me. Of course, I can't really see her either. Not really. Although sometimes I… It's almost as if I could see her, sometimes. If I concentrate very hard it's like I can just glimpse her out of the corner of my eye.

(She is thoughtful for a second) Still. Anyway. I've kept Zara for years and years. Until they all started saying I was much too old for that sort of thing and got worried and started talking about sending for a doctor. So then I didn't take her round with me quite so much after that. But she's still here. And when I feel really sad and depressed like I do today, then I sit and talk to Zara. Zara always understands. Zara always listens. She's special. Aren't you, Zara?

(She listens to Zara) What's that? Yes, I wish he'd turn his music down, too. I've asked him, haven't I? *(mimicking Gary)* 'How can I hear it if I turn it down, I can't hear the bass then, can I?' I used to have pictures in here but every time he put a disc on they fell off the walls.

(Pause. The music continues) I mean, don't get me wrong. We like loud music, don't we Zara? We love loud music. Sometimes.

(Yelling) BUT NOT ALL THE TIME.

(Pause)

Why doesn't he ever listen to quiet music? Just once? Wouldn't that be nice? […] But if he did that, he wouldn't be Grisly Gary then, would he?

(Pause)

Oh, Zara, did I tell you I've been picked for the school swimming team? Isn't that exciting? Yes. Thank you. I'm glad you're excited, too. Good.

(Pause)

(Shouting) IF ANYONE IS INTERESTED AT ALL, I WAS PICKED FOR THE SCHOOL SWIMMING TEAM TODAY. WHAT ABOUT THAT, FOLKS?

(She listens. No reply)

Great. Thanks for your support, everyone. *(tearful)* They might at least… They could have at least… Oh, Zara… I know you're always here, but sometimes I get so… lonely…

(She sits on her bed, sad, angry and frustrated)

Alan Ayckbourn, from *Invisible Friends*

Monologue B

Valere, a vain actor has just been criticised by a fellow performer. When Valere asks for written critiques, the other actor asks why; this monologue is Valere's response. NB This play is set in 1654, but was written in 1991. The playwright stresses that 'The pace is frantic'.

VALERE:

Because I'm anxious to *improve*!
Is that so strange, my wanting to remove
The flaws from my persona? Surely not!
I loathe a blemish! I despise a spot!
Perfection is the goal towards which I strive
(For me, that's what it means to be alive)
And, hence, I'm grateful for a shrewd critique:
It keeps my talent honest, so to speak!
We of the theatre share that common view –
The criticisms of the things we do
Inspire our interest, not our hurt or rage:
We know it's part of "being on the stage"
To have oneself assessed at every turn,
And thus we show a willingness to learn
From judgements which might wound another man.
I much prefer to any drooling fan
A critic who will SLICE me into parts!
GOD LOVE THE CRITICS! *BLESS* THEIR PICKY HEARTS!
Precisely, and in no uncertain terms,
They halve the apple, showing us our worms.

David Hirson, from *La Bête*

2. Write down your initial thoughts about each monologue. What insights are you given into the characters? Think about:
   - what we find out about their situation or context
   - what emotions each character displays.

3. How does the structure and layout of the language help us to understand the character? Think about:

- whether the language is formal or informal
- whether the layout on the page suggests a rhythm
- whether the punctuation indicates particular emotions (such as calm or anxiety).

4. Now, copy and complete the following table referring to the style of each monologue. Tick the boxes that apply in each case.

Monologue	A	B
Contemporary		
Classical		
Verse		
Prose		
Fast pace		
Slow pace		
Comic		
Tragic		
To the audience		
To other characters		

DEVELOPING THE SKILLS

Now that you have explored both texts, choose either monologue A or B as one you are going to work with.

5. Reread your chosen monologue. Now, use a table like the one below to write down any emotions shown by the speaker and how they change over the course of the speeches. For example, for Monologue A, does Lucy start off her monologue in a bright and cheerful manner, or sullen and angry?

Starting emotion	Any changes in between	Final emotion

6. How would you like the audience to feel when watching your performance? Do you want them to empathise and identify with the character, or to feel hatred and scorn? Write a short paragraph describing your intention for the monologue.

 REFLECTIVE LOG Identify reasons that you have chosen the monologue and how you feel about the speaker. What do you think is important to bring out and highlight for your audience?

You can now begin to develop your characterisation. This will be based on factual information you have found out (such as the character's age, family situation and so on) as well as your own interpretation of them (what sort of person you think they are).

7. Look at the diagram below. Copy and complete this, adding in information about the character and your own ideas. Notice the links that can be made between the different areas, and add more links of your own.

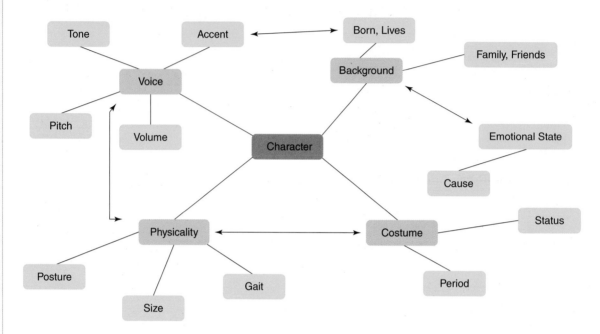

8. Ask a friend to hot-seat you – they can ask you questions that you must answer spontaneously in character. Write down any extra character information that you produce.

With a developed understanding of the character and the context of the monologue, you can now shape and structure it. Think of the speech like a piece of music, with crescendos (parts that get louder), diminuendos (parts that get quieter), pauses and varying pace. You can orchestrate the piece carefully to achieve the most effective emotional response.

9. Now draw a graph that represents the monologue. Plot the 'peaks and troughs' of emotional intensity so that you can visualise the shape of the piece.

Blocking will also help you to create the mood you want.

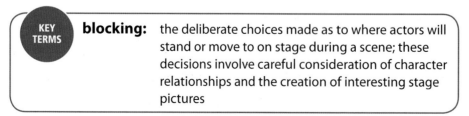

KEY TERMS

blocking: the deliberate choices made as to where actors will stand or move to on stage during a scene; these decisions involve careful consideration of character relationships and the creation of interesting stage pictures

10. Focus on a small section of your monologue. What blocking do you think should be used? Think about:

- your character's physicality at this moment
- whether your character should be sitting, standing, or moving (or move between all these)
- when moments of stillness might be more effective than movement.

11. Now look at this example, based on monologue B, of one student's annotation of part of the script:

> **VALERE:**
> The criticisms of the things we do
> Inspire our <u>interest</u>, not our <u>hurt</u> or <u>rage</u>:
> We know it's part of "<u>being on the stage</u>"
> To have oneself <u>assessed</u> at <u>every turn</u>,
> And thus we show a willingness to learn
> From judgements which might wound another man.
> I much prefer to any <u>drooling</u> <u>fan</u>
> A critic who will <u>SLICE</u> me into parts!
> GOD *LOVE* THE CRITICS! *BLESS* THEIR PICKY HEARTS!

Annotation
Emphasise sarcasm, focus on contrast between 'interest', 'hurt' and 'rage'. Last two said with bitter, hissing tone
Use large, flourishing movements and proud vocal tone to highlight more sarcasm
Bring out the words 'assessed' and 'every turn' by focusing on consonants, hissing again
Emphasise 'drooling fan' by elongating the 'oo' sound of the word and relaxing muscles to produce fluid, pathetic movement
Move swiftly towards other actor, use sharp, chopping hand gesture to indicate a sudden 'slice'. 'Slice' spoken much louder than other words, start to build up intensity for climax on next line
Biggest climax in volume and emotion, with an angry, sarcastic tone and large open physicality

12. What blocking have they put in place?

13. In what ways could they have been more precise?

APPLYING THE SKILLS

14. Now, annotate your own selected section of your monologue in the same way, identifying and drawing out the emotions, intentions and character interpretations you have worked on.

15. Finally, perform either the whole monologue, or this selected part of it.

CHECKLIST FOR SUCCESS

✓ Use emotional changes to guide your performance
✓ Think about how you can block the piece to develop the story of the monologue
✓ Communicate meaning through facial expressions, physicality and vocal skills

---

SOUND PROGRESS

- I can confidently deliver a monologue that is clear and well structured.

EXCELLENT PROGRESS

- I can develop a detailed characterisation and interpretation for my well-structured monologue.

5.4 Exploring group scripts

LEARNING OBJECTIVES

- Learn approaches to start exploring and rehearsing an extract for performance
- Consider ways to shape scenes and interact on stage, developing meaning and impact

SPOTLIGHT ON How can my group rehearse our script effectively?

STARTING POINT

Rehearsing and performing a script as part of a group requires a range of key skills and areas to focus on:

- personal, individual preparation of character (as in Unit 5.3)
- the relationship that your character has with others on stage (in plot and through proxemics)
- the plot, purpose and shape of the scene itself (make sure everyone in your group has read the whole play)
- emotional content, **subtext**, intention and meaning
- the social, historical and possibly political context of the play itself.

KEY TERMS **subtext:** underlying meaning within dialogue or a scene; often the unspoken, real motives or thoughts of a character

1. Have you worked on a group script before? What did you find difficult or challenging? What worked well?

EXPLORING THE SKILLS

Although there is a lot to think about, there are some approaches to rehearsal that will allow the key elements to fall into place naturally as you explore the piece. However, the following is just one way to approach the process.

2. Begin by reading the following scene from *The Madness of George III* by Alan Bennett. Do it first on your own and then aloud with the rest of your group. The cast read-through, in particular, will help spark initial thoughts and ideas for characterisation and interpretation.

In this scene, King George meets Willis for the first time and has just been delivering a long 'mad', rambling speech. Willis has been employed to try and cure the king of his illness.

KING *slowly circles* WILLIS, *looking at him keenly but with no change in his tone.*

KING: We can plough a furrow, you know, give us a field, a decent plough and we could plough you a furrow as straight as a ruler, straight as a ruler done by a ruler, and another beside it and another beside that until you had as pretty a ploughed field as you could find this side of Cirencester. Put us out of our kingdom tomorrow and I would not want for employment.

WILLIS: I have a farm.

KING: Give me the management of fifty acres and ploughing and sowing and harvest, and I could do it and make me a handsome profit into the bargain.

WILLIS: I said I have a farm, Your Majesty.

The KING *stops, looks at him.*

GREVILLE: This gentleman, sir, has made the illness under which Your Majesty labours his special study.

WILLIS: (*To* GREVILLE) Hush, sir.

KING: A mad doctor, is it? I am not mad, just nervous.

WILLIS: I will endeavour to alleviate some of the inconveniences from which Your Majesty suffers.

KING: Inconveniences? Insults. Assaults. And salts beside rubbed into these wounds, sir. See. (WILLIS *loosens the bandages to look at the sores on his legs.*) I eat my meals with a spoon, sir. A pusher. George by the Grace of God King of England, Ireland, Scotland, Elector of Hanover, Duke of Brunswick. A pusher. By your dress, sir, and general demeanour I would say you were a minister of God.

WILLIS: That is true, Your Majesty. I was once in the service of the Church, now I practise medicine.

KING: Then I am sorry for it. You have quitted a profession I have always loved, and embraced one I most heartily detest.

WILLIS: Our Saviour went about healing the sick.

KING: Yes, but he had not £700 a year for it.
(GREVILLE *and the* PAGES *laugh.* WILLIS *does not laugh.*)
Yes, but he had not £700 a year for it, eh? Not bad for a madman.

WILLIS: I have a hospital in Lincolnshire, sir.

KING: I know Lincolnshire. Fine sheep. Admirable sheep. There are pigs, too. Pigs can be very fine. Hay is the means of maintenance of the cow, grass of the sheep, oats of the horse, and pigs will eat anything. I have a fondness for pigs. But I know of no hospitals.

WILLIS: We have cows and sheep and pigs also.

KING: In the hospital? Are they mad too?

WILLIS: My patients work, sir. They till the soil. They cultivate and in so doing they acquire a better conceit of themselves.

KING: I am King of England, sir. A man can have no better conceit of himself than that.

(WILLIS *suddenly takes hold of the* KING's *shoulder, and the* KING *freezes.* FITZROY, GREVILLE *and the PAGES are plainly shocked and the* KING *rigid with anger.* WILLIS *deliberately looks the* KING *in the eye.*)

KING: Do you look at me, sir?

WILLIS: I do, sir.

KING: I have you in my eye.

WILLIS: No. I have you in my eye.

KING: You are bold, but by God I am bolder.

(*The* KING *suddenly goes for* WILLIS *but* WILLIS *dodges and the force of the rush makes the* KING *fall down. He remains sitting on the ground, while* WILLIS *lectures him.*)

WILLIS: You can control your utterance, sir, if you would. I believe you can be well if only you will.

KING: Do not look at me. I am not one of your farmers.

WILLIS: Your Majesty must behave, or endeavour to do so.

KING: (*Still struggling*) Must, must? Whose must? Your must or my must? No must. Get away from me.

PAPANDIEK: Easy sir, easy.

KING: (*As they try to get him up*) No, no. Leave me, boys. Let me sit upon the ground and tell…tell-tell-tell-tell…tell this lump-headed fool to shut his gob box. You…

WILLIS: Clean your tongue, sir. Clean your tongue.

GRENVILLE: Hush, sir.

PAPANDIEK: Be still, sir.

KING: I will not be still. I will be a guest in the graveyard first.

WILLIS: Very well. If Your Majesty does not behave, you must be restrained.

(WILLIS *opens the door and three of his servants, grim-faced and in leather aprons, wheel in the restraining chair, a wooden contraption with clamps for the arms and legs and a band for the head. The sight of the restraining chair momentarily silences the* KING.)

KING: When felons were induced to talk they were first shown the instrument of their torture. The King is shown the instrument of his to induce him not to talk. Well, I won't, I won't. Not for you or anyone.

(*The* KING *begins abusing them again, with a torrent of obscenity, as, quietly at first, but growing louder as the scene comes to its climax, we hear Handel's Coronation Anthem, Zadok the Priest. One servant thrusts aside the protesting PAGES while the other two lift the* KING *up and amid the ensuing pandemonium manhandle him into the restraining chair.*)

See them off boys! See them off! (*As he is hauled to the chair*) Damn you. I'll have you all thrashed for this! Horse-whipped. Lie off, you rascals. Lie off.

Shut up, you sanctimonious fool.

FITZROY: This is unseemly, sir. Who are these ruffians?

GRENVILLE: You have no business, sir. His Majesty is ill.

BRAUN: Go easy, my old love.

PAPANDIEK: Steady, Your Majesty, steady. Leave off, leave off.

FITZROY: I must inform His Royal Highness. This is a scandal.

GRENVILLE: Call off your dogs, sir. Who are these barkers?

WILLIS: If the King refuses food he will be restrained. If he claims to have no appetite he will be restrained. If he swears and indulges in meaningless discourse he will be restrained. If he throws off his bedclothes, tears away his bandages, scratches at his sores, and if he does not strive every day and always towards his own recovery, then he must be restrained.

(WILLIS's *men stand back from the* KING *and we see that he has been strapped into the chair, feet and arms clamped, his head held rigid by a band round his forehead.*)

KING: (*Howling*) I am the King of England.

WILLIS: No, sir. You are the patient.

(*The Coronation Anthem finally reaches its climax and bursts forth in the chorus of* Zadok the Priest, *as the* KING *struggles, howling, in the chair, with* WILLIS's *men lined up behind him.*)

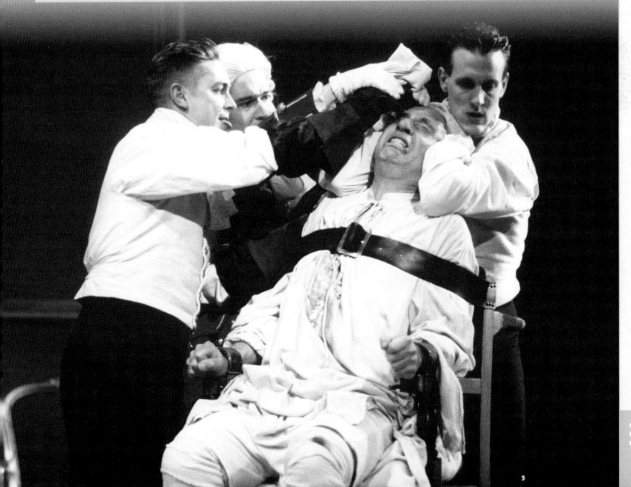

3. Now, research some key aspects that will help with your group's performance of the extract. Each member of your group could take one of these areas: historical, political and social context; the playwright; the plot; other performances of the play; images.

4. Then, discuss the following points with your group:

- What are your and your fellow cast members' initial thoughts about the extract?
- What is happening in this scene and why is it important?
- What is the context, both within the play and within history or society?
- What has changed or developed for your character in this extract and indeed in the play as a whole up to this moment?
- How does the specific inclusion of sound (the music) help to shape the scene?
- What impact should this scene have on stage and why?
- What overall themes do you see as being explored here?

DEVELOPING THE SKILLS

In order to develop a piece that makes sense and has a 'shape' to it, you need to break the piece down before putting it all together again. 'Marking the moment' is one key way of shaping the performance.

5. Begin by identifying key moments within the scene that you feel are important to highlight: for example, moments when there are changes in emotion, pace or intensity.

It will help to choose one from the very beginning and the final moment, with three fairly evenly spaced moments in between. Once you have made your choice, copy and complete this table. (Two suggestions have been made for you but you may want to adapt or change these.)

1	The King's speech
2	
3	
4	
5	King strapped into the chair with Willis's men behind him

6. Now create a still image or tableau for each of these moments. Try to capture the emotions and intentions of each character within these images. Use proxemics, thinking carefully about constructing the tableaux for maximum impact. Experiment with:

- levels
- facial expressions
- variety in physicality and actions.

Your aim is to capture the feel of the entire extract by presenting the tableaux in sequence, creating a smooth, silent overview of the scene. By exploring the focal moments in this way, you and your group will begin to develop a shape and sense of modulation within the piece. Rooting the piece initially in these important moments will help you to develop tension and emotional peaks.

REFLECTIVE LOG
Jot down any decisions that your group made about the key characters, themes and intentions, and remind yourselves of these features as you rehearse. Check that you remain true to these or notice and log if opinions change and develop.

7. Now run through the scene with dialogue, but each time you reach one of your moments, hold the tableau for four seconds before continuing with the scene. Once you have tried this technique, makes notes about anything that worked particularly well and whether there was anything that needed to change.

APPLYING THE SKILLS

You have worked on some selected moments from your scene, but now it is time to prepare the entire extract.

8. As a group, decide on some general blocking of the scene. You have read about the way that stage configuration and design can aid you in projecting your message, so agree on the stage layout first. As you rehearse you should not be afraid to confirm, tighten up or change areas if something is not working.

9. Now, take the script a section at a time and annotate carefully as you rehearse. An example is given below. Think about:

- blocking
- proxemics
- balance on the stage
- variety of action, movement, physicality and facial expressions
- the moments you previously marked as important.

King to centre left by end of line in time for Willis's grab. Follow script stage directions for reactions

Tension high, King moves quickly around stage, Willis remains static and calm centre stage, Pages stand to attention upstage left

KING: I am King of England, sir. A man can have no better conceit of himself than that.

WILLIS *suddenly takes hold of the* KING's *shoulder, and the* KING *freezes.* FITZROY, GREVILLE *and the* PAGES *are plainly shocked and the* KING *rigid with anger.* WILLIS *deliberately looks the* KING *in the eye.*

Firm, controlled tone of voice, upright stance, chin high, resolute

KING: Do you look at me, sir?

WILLIS: I do, sir.

KING: I have you in my eye.

WILLIS: No. I have you in my eye.

KING: You are bold, but by God I am bolder.

King screams line, enraged – Pages react, make as if to move, but think better of it

Narrowed eyes, suspicious, angry tone, almost low growl

Pause before line, nonchalant tone, stance remains same

King relaxes slightly, draws himself up to full height, calm before he launches

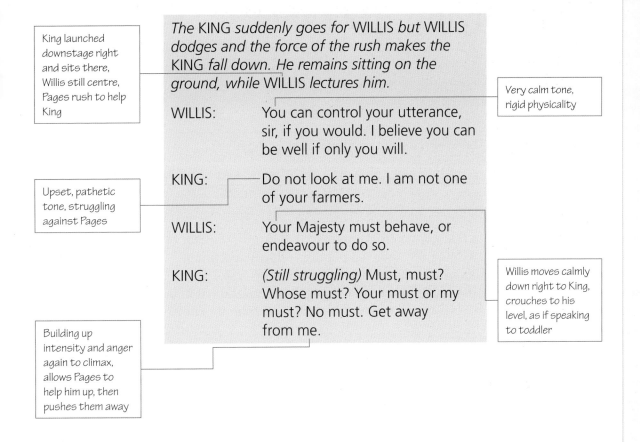

King launched downstage right and sits there, Willis still centre, Pages rush to help King

The KING suddenly goes for WILLIS but WILLIS dodges and the force of the rush makes the KING fall down. He remains sitting on the ground, while WILLIS lectures him.

Very calm tone, rigid physicality

WILLIS: You can control your utterance, sir, if you would. I believe you can be well if only you will.

KING: Do not look at me. I am not one of your farmers.

Upset, pathetic tone, struggling against Pages

WILLIS: Your Majesty must behave, or endeavour to do so.

KING: *(Still struggling)* Must, must? Whose must? Your must or my must? No must. Get away from me.

Willis moves calmly down right to King, crouches to his level, as if speaking to toddler

Building up intensity and anger again to climax, allows Pages to help him up, then pushes them away

10. Finally, perform your script as a group, using what you have learned to guide you.

CHECKLIST FOR SUCCESS

✓ Demonstrate your understanding of the context and intention of the scene in your preparation and performance
✓ Make sure your own character is fully developed so that you can interact in a meaningful way with others on stage
✓ Include 'light and shade' in your performance, by building up times of emotional climax or by softening the gentler moments

SOUND PROGRESS

• I can rehearse and perform a well-constructed scene with my group, giving a clear sense of plot and character development.

EXCELLENT PROGRESS

• I can confidently perform a scene that demonstrates my knowledge of subtext and meaning, by identifying and developing key moments and themes within the piece.

5.5 Applying the skills

* Apply the skills you have learned to a monologue

> **SPOTLIGHT ON** How do I bring all my script performance skills together?

STARTING POINT

Read this monologue that comes from the play, *A Raisin in the Sun* by Lorraine Hansberry. Walter, 35, shares a poor, run-down apartment with his wife Ruth, his son Travis aged 10 or 11, and his sister and mother. His mother has given him her savings to put into the bank, but he has decided to invest it with a somewhat unreliable man he knows.

Travis:	What you gonna do tonight, Daddy?
Walter:	You wouldn't understand yet, son, but your daddy's gonna make a transaction... a business transaction that's gonna change our lives... that's how come one day when you 'bout seventeen years old I'll come home and I'll be pretty tired, you know what I mean, after a day of conferences and secretaries getting things wrong the way they do... 'cause an executive's life is hell, man – (*The more he talks, the further away he gets.*) And I'll pull the car up on the driveway... just a plain black Chrysler, I think with white walls – no – black tires. More elegant. Rich people don't have to be flashy... though I'll get something a little sportier for Ruth – maybe a Cadillac convertible to do her shopping in... And I'll come up the steps to the house and the gardener will be clipping away at the hedges and I'll say 'Hello, Jefferson, how are you this evening?' And I'll go inside and Ruth will come downstairs and meet me at the door and we'll kiss each other, she'll take my arm and we'll go up to your room to see you sitting on the floor with the catalogues of all the great schools in America around you... All the great schools in the world! And – and I'll say, all right son – it's your seventeenth birthday, what is it you've decided?... Just tell me, what is it you want to be – and you'll be it... Whatever you want to be – Yessir!

EXPLORING THE SKILLS

1. Make some initial notes on:

* your impressions of Walter
* his situation and intentions (what he hopes will happen)
* the overall form and style of his speech (is it classical, modern, formal, informal?)
* who Walter is speaking to (his son, the audience, both or neither?)
* any particular words, phrases or sections that stand out.

Try to draw on the ideas you learned about in Unit 5.3.

DEVELOPING THE SKILLS

The context of the speech is useful for your interpretation. Walter has already expressed his desire to invest in a scheme run by a friend, but his wife and mother both see it as foolhardy. The play also takes place between World War II and the mid 1950s, a time of opportunity for many Americans who dreamed of making something of themselves. However, these opportunities were not always open to black people.

2. Now develop a fuller picture of Walter. Use the spider diagram format from Unit 5.3 or simply write a sentence or two about each of these elements below:

   - Walter's emotional state
   - his physicality (how you think he will move, use space)
   - his voice
   - how he might be dressed – his costume
   - his background/life and how this might affect your performance.

3. Next, annotate a copy of the speech, adding your ideas to it. Think about tone of voice, movements, gestures and how you will block the speech, and what intentions you have in terms of communicating meaning to the audience. Are there opportunities for you to contrast pace (e.g. slow to fast), intensity and lightness, or humour and sadness?

> in control, but excited: moves towards son, centre stage left – pulls up chair and sits, looks at Travis directly

You wouldn't understand yet, son, but your daddy's gonna make a transaction ...

> conspiratorial: looks over his shoulders, as if to check if anyone is listening

REFLECTIVE LOG Do your own research into *A Raisin in the Sun* and make some basic notes on the story as a whole and its key themes. If you can, try to read a copy of the play.

APPLYING THE SKILLS

4. Now prepare your monologue and perform it for a group or your class as a whole.

CHECKLIST FOR SUCCESS

✓ Break down the speech into significant, 'marked' moments that signal changes in emotion
✓ Try to convey your own understanding of both Walter's character and the style of the piece
✓ Create emotional impact and moments of change, and introduce both light and shade

SOUND PROGRESS

- I can identify a basic characterisation for a monologue and convey a clear idea of my chosen character.

EXCELLENT PROGRESS

- I can develop a detailed and thoughtful representation of my character and create the intended impact on my audience.

CHECK YOUR PROGRESS

Use these statements as a way of evaluating your progress throughout this chapter.

SOUND PROGRESS ✓

- ☐ I can identify the differences between styles of written play.
- ☐ I can draw my own conclusions about the style of a play and imagine it on stage.
- ☐ I can confidently deliver a monologue that is clear and well structured.
- ☐ I can rehearse and perform a well-constructed scene with my group, giving a clear sense of plot and character development.
- ☐ I can identify a basic characterisation for a monologue and convey a clear idea of my chosen character.

EXCELLENT PROGRESS ✓

- ☐ I can infer detailed ideas about styles, action and tone from a range of plays.
- ☐ I can infer ideas about a play's genre and style, consider a number of options and use this to make my own interpretation.
- ☐ I can develop a detailed characterisation and interpretation for my well-structured monologue.
- ☐ I can confidently perform a scene that demonstrates my knowledge of subtext and meaning, by identifying and developing key moments and themes within the piece.
- ☐ I can develop a detailed and thoughtful representation of my character and create the intended impact on my audience.

EXTENDED SCRIPTS

STARTING POINTS

In this chapter you are going to develop a range of skills related to responding to tasks on a longer script.

You will learn how to:

- consider possible approaches and interpretations when working on a longer script

- focus on specific elements within a longer script and learn about the different skills required to address them

- express ideas in your responses in succinct yet informed ways

- read and evaluate example students' responses to a longer script.

CHAPTER CONTENTS

The activities you complete will primarily relate to written responses to extended scripts, but you will also participate in other practical activities as a way of engaging with the scripts themselves.

You will:

- read and respond with practical activities to extracts from the play *Humble Boy* by Charlotte Jones

- write two short written responses about suggested acting approaches for characters in *Humble Boy*

- consider how particular props might be used in *Humble Boy* and what their function might be

- trace a character's development in *Humble Boy* across a longer extract and sustain a written response about the character, addressing a wide range of performance aspects

- read and explore an extract from the play *Strife* by John Galsworthy

- evaluate a range of responses to *Strife* in relation to costume design and the role of two of the characters

- keep a reflective log in which you record what you have done and reflect on, or evaluate, key aspects of your work.

6.1 Exploring a longer script

LEARNING OBJECTIVES

- Explore the opening to a longer script
- Consider possible interpretations and approaches

> **SPOTLIGHT ON**
> How can I break down a longer script so that I can engage with its ideas and structures?

STARTING POINT

When tackling a longer script, you will need to use many, if not all, of the techniques and approaches you have worked on throughout this book. Above all, it is vital to give the script itself a detailed and thoughtful reading, trying to engage with key ideas in it.

Read the following opening to the play *Humble Boy* by Charlotte Jones. This is an abridged (that is, shortened) version.

1. As you read it, make some basic notes about what seem to be the central **motifs** or ideas running through it.

> **KEY TERMS**
> **motif:** a symbol, image, or turn of phrase that crops up repeatedly in a text

The context of the play

First performed in 2001, *Humble Boy* deals with the ramifications of the death of James Humble, whose funeral precedes the opening scene. His son, Felix, aged 35, has returned home and has arrived at the family house. The play explores grief and absence, and underlying conflict in family relationships. It also has strong echoes of William Shakespeare's play, *Hamlet*. This extract concerns three of the cast: Felix, his mother Flora, and her friend, Mercy.

Scene One

Set: a pretty country garden. Perhaps the suggestions of a house or a glass conservatory from which the characters enter into the garden. A patio area, perhaps with a path through the garden. At the back there is an area for gardening tools; a gardening chair or stool. There is a garden hosepipe wound up there. Something of a lawn with borders. A rose bush. At the end of the garden there is a large beehive. The suggestion of an apple tree – perhaps just some overhanging branches with a few apples.

The stage is in darkness. There is music. Perhaps resonant of 'The Flight of the Bumblebee'. The beehive lights up to suggest the bees leaving the hive. The lights fade

---

up on the rest of the garden. The music is still playing and the hive continues to throb with light.

Felix Humble walks in a stumbling, uncertain way into the garden. He is transfixed by the hive. He is an overweight but not unattractive man of about 35. He wears old and slightly greying cricket clothes, despite the fact that he is not a sportsman by any stretch of the imagination. He climbs up the steps and takes off the lid of the hive and looks in. The music ends.

Mercy Lott enters the garden. She is wearing black clothes with brown shoes. She is in her late fifties, a petite and timid, mousy woman. She watches Felix with concern. She approaches him but doesn't get too close. Felix glances at her; then returns his attention to the hive.

Felix:	(*he stumbles on the letter 'b'*) The b–b–b–bees have gone.
Mercy:	Yes, dear. Will you come in now?
Felix:	They took the b–bees away. I saw them.
Mercy:	Your mother isn't cross. She just wants you to come in.
Felix:	There were four of them. The bee-keepers. All in white.
Mercy:	I'm sure if you just say a little sorry to her –
Felix:	They looked like astronauts.
Mercy:	Did they?
Felix:	Or cosmonauts. Depending.
Mercy:	On what, dear?
Felix:	If we were in Russia.

[...]

Felix puts the lid back on and climbs slowly and awkwardly down.

Felix:	What do you call a group of b–bee-keepers, Mercy?
Mercy:	Is this a joke? I'm not very good with jokes, dear.
Felix:	No, I mean what's the word? Like a flock of sheep. A herd of cows, a pack of dogs, a – a jubilation of larks.
Mercy:	Is it really? A jubilation. How lovely.
Felix:	What is it for b–bee-keepers?
Mercy:	Do you know? I've no idea.
Felix:	What is it for astronauts? A group of astronauts?
Mercy:	Shall we discuss it inside, dear?
Felix:	Something to do with them being white. And weightless. And silent.
Mercy:	We shouldn't leave your mother on her own with all the others.
Felix:	I just have to find the right word.

[...]

Flora enters. She is a very attractive woman in her late fifties. She looks young for her age. She wears a stylish navy blue dress and Jackie Onassis[1] sunglasses.

Mercy:	Flora! We were just coming in. Weren't we, Felix? We were just sorting out what you call a group of bee-keepers and then we were right with you. Do you need me to do more sandwiches? She's not angry. You're not angry, are you Flora?
Flora:	No.
Mercy:	There. I told you she wasn't angry. We can all go in now. Your mother isn't angry with you.
Felix:	Yes she is.
Flora:	*(calmly)* I am not angry, Felix. I am incandescent with rage.
Mercy:	Oh dear.
Felix:	*(stammering badly)* An apocalypse of b–b–b–b–bee-keepers. What do you think of that for a collective noun, Mother? It's not b–b–bad, is it?
Flora:	Stop that, Felix. You haven't done that since you were at prep school.[2]
Mercy:	He's just a little jittery.
Flora:	He's doing it to annoy me.
Mercy:	I'm sure he's not – you're not, are you, Felix?
Flora:	He can speak perfectly well, if he wants to. He's doing it on purpose.
Felix:	*(extreme frustration)* I'm trying to b–b–b–b–b–
Mercy:	*(supplying the word for him)* Behave? He's trying to behave, Flora.

△ Actors portraying the characters
of Flora and Felix

Flora:	*(coolly)* I'm afraid, Felix, you will not get the sympathy vote. Today your father has a prior claim.
Felix:	I saw them, Mother. The apocalypse of b–b–b– *(He gives up)*. They were here. While my father was being consigned to dust. You got rid of them immediately. His be– his be– be–
Flora:	I got rid of the bees on professional advice. They were swarming. Since your father's death they have developed very alarming tendencies.
Felix:	P–perhaps they were angry.
Mercy:	Felix.
Felix:	I came home and I went through the house and I find all my father's be–be–be– all his things gone. All his clothes.
Mercy:	Flora very kindly gave them to me. For the Romanian orphans.
Flora:	His bee-keeping suit is still there. In the garage. It is a constant reminder.
Mercy:	I could have taken it but Jean who runs the shop was worried there wouldn't be much call.
Felix:	I come home – and there is just an absence.
Flora:	Don't question what I do, Felix. You weren't here.
Felix:	I'm trying to find the right words.
Flora:	Oh yes, Felix. You carry on. That is what this day has been lacking. Yes. There we all were, waiting in the church for you to find just the right words. Waiting for my clever son, my golden boy, the Cambridge don[3], to deliver his father's oration.

[1] Jackie Onassis: formerly the glamorous wife of John F Kennedy, President of the USA in the 60s.
[2] prep school: private, independent (fee-paying) school for young children
[3] Cambridge don: senior academic lecturer at Cambridge University

EXPLORING THE SKILLS

On the surface, this appears to be a fairly realistic play. The concerns are everyday – the funeral of a family member, the return of the deceased's son, discussions about the father's belongings. But there are elements that point towards more elevated, almost spiritual ideas:

- the idea of absence – of someone not being there but still there somehow
- the focus on nature and the garden, which often symbolises wider or more profound ideas
- ideas to do with names of things, meanings, trying to express oneself – the title of the play is *Humble Boy* which sounds similar to 'bumble bee'.

2. How are each of these things touched on in the extract? Write a paragraph on each one, giving one example of how each of these motifs or concerns arises in the text. For example:

> The idea of absence is introduced in a number of ways. Firstly, there is the obvious absence of Felix's father, who is discussed but does not appear...

A second core element that contributes to the play's effect is the characterisation.

There are three distinct characters whom we meet in the flesh in the opening.

3. How does Charlotte Jones suggest their distinctness to the audience? Copy and complete this table about each one:

Character	Appearance/clothing	Their entrance on stage	Manner / tone of speech
Felix	Overweight, wearing old cricket clothes	'in a stumbling, uncertain way'	
Mercy		Has come to look for Felix (sent by Flora?) but doesn't come too close to him	
Flora	Glamorous, attractive, designer style		

From these descriptions it is almost inevitable that there is going to be conflict. For example, in different ways, one could say that both Felix and his mother are dressed inappropriately for a funeral.

4. What reasons have Felix and Flora got for being annoyed with each other?

5. What is Mercy's role in this situation?

6. How would your understanding of the **dynamic** between the three of them affect how this scene would be played?

KEY TERMS

dynamic: the forces in a relationship that create change or reactions

REFLECTIVE LOG

Make some initial notes on your ideas for how the scene would be played, identifying the ways in which the characters speak and seem to behave. Make sure you update these notes in the light of the work below.

DEVELOPING THE SKILLS

In order to engage fully with the script, however, you need to pay sustained, detailed attention to it in a range of ways.

Look at the opening from the moment Felix enters up to and including his line 'They looked like astronauts'.

7. Working with a partner, discuss your views on the characters of both Felix and Mercy. Go back to your completed table from Task 3 and look for any other clues about movement. Consider the proxemics – where does Mercy stand during this dialogue? Does she move? What about Felix?

8. Try out a number of different ways of playing the lines, all the time with the thought in your heads – what are we trying to achieve? What are we trying to say to the audience?

What core ideas do you want to get across? Felix's sadness, or is it anger – or a mixture of both? Mercy's inability to connect with him, or her kindness, or both?

Go back to all you have learned about status, gesture and speech and apply it to these few short lines.

APPLYING THE SKILLS

Now, complete this short task about those lines:

9. Give two pieces of advice to the actors playing Felix and Mercy in this short section on how to perform.

CHECKLIST FOR SUCCESS

✓ Link your comments on how actors should perform to the script and the ideas you have distilled from analysing it
✓ Apply an appropriate and useful range of dramatic techniques and terms to your explanation

SOUND PROGRESS

• I can identify the ways in which the characters are different or distinctive and make some basic suggestions about their performances.

EXCELLENT PROGRESS

• I can write clearly and confidently about performances, linking my proposals to the text itself and making relevant inferences from the evidence.

Responding to specific aspects of the script

- Consider how specific aspects of performance, design or directorial work might be applied to a longer script

> **SPOTLIGHT ON** How can I tackle tasks that require me to focus on very specific parts of a script?

STARTING POINT

Written scripts often provide detailed guidance on sets, what characters wear and what props they use (when essential to the plot). Nevertheless, there is a vast empty space for you as performer, director or designer, to make your mark on someone else's script.

Take the opening two lines from *Humble Boy*:

Felix:	*(he stumbles on the letter 'b')* The b–b–b–bees have gone.
Mercy:	Yes, dear. Will you come in now?

We know that it is the day of Felix's father's funeral and that his mother is hosting a reception for the people who attended the funeral. They are inside, whereas Felix and Mercy are in the garden. Mercy has come to fetch him. We also know the writer has described her as timid.

1. What might she have been doing before she came onto the stage? Think about these suggestions:

| serving food | making tea | collecting glasses | looking around the house for Felix |

Or perhaps something else? We can't know for sure, and you would need to read the whole play to get a full sense of Mercy's character, but on the evidence here it is likely she has been helping Felix's mother in some way.

2. With this in mind, what prop might Mercy be holding?

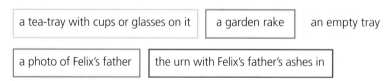

| a tea-tray with cups or glasses on it | a garden rake | an empty tray |

| a photo of Felix's father | the urn with Felix's father's ashes in |

Some of these are possible; others unlikely. An item with a lot of significance is likely to be mentioned in the script, so if Mercy does have a prop, it is likely to be one that supports her role, rather than becomes a key element in the plot.

EXPLORING THE SKILLS

When props are used, there need to be valid reasons for them. Here a student explains his suggestion of how a prop might be used by Felix in these opening lines.

> I think when Felix goes up to the hive, he sees a pair of gardening gloves on the stool that the writer mentions. I think he will see these are his father's, pick them up, look at them for a moment – and then put them down, before looking into the hive. It will emphasise the connection of the bees, and the garden, with Felix's father and the idea of loss.

3. What prop does the student suggest might be used here?

4. What reason does the student provide for the use of the prop? Do you think it is a good one? Why?

5. Now, have a look back at the whole of the scene given in Unit 6.1.

   Can you think of another occasion in this scene when a prop might be used effectively? Reread the set directions again to see if there is anything mentioned by the writer you could use (such as an apple from the apple tree?).

   Write a paragraph explaining:

   • what the prop is and how it would be used effectively
   • your reasons for its use.

Bear in mind what the prop's purpose is – think of it as having three potential roles:

Functional	Atmospheric	Symbolic
It is simply used as part of the action: for example, a tray may be needed if a lot of glasses are to be collected.	The prop may or may not be used, but it adds to the 'feel' or mood of the scene or action. It might give information about the story and situation (like the tray of cups and glasses indicating a social event).	It has a wider role, perhaps to further establish character or provide contrast between characters, or to emphasise or draw attention to a theme or key idea.

If you are stuck for ideas, you could consider one of the following:

| an apple | | 'Order of Service' from the funeral | | a glass of water |

| a gardening trowel | | a book or newspaper | | a piece of luggage |

| a fly swatter | | a cup of coffee |

DEVELOPING THE SKILLS

A similar approach can be used when you are responding to questions about particular characters. Let us look at Flora's character and how she might be played in these lines:

Felix:	I'm trying to find the right words.
Flora:	Oh yes, Felix. You carry on. That is what this day has been lacking. Yes. There we all were, waiting in the church for you to find just the right words. Waiting for my clever son, my golden boy, the Cambridge don, to deliver his father's oration.

Start by establishing what we know about Flora, Felix's mother, at this point:

- She is incandescent with rage (extremely angry because Felix failed to speak at his father's funeral and is now outside rather than talking with the guests)
- She is glamorous, and her appearance contrasts strongly with Felix's rather tatty clothing.

6. Briefly read her lines aloud, then consider:

- her tone of voice – is she being genuinely complimentary when she says 'my clever son'?
- her emphasis on particular words – which ones would she stress most? Why?
- her posture – if Felix is possibly bumbling around, trying to speak, how might she stand in contrast to him?
- her facial expressions and gestures – how does someone show anger?

7. Discuss your ideas with a partner. Then have another go at reading the exchange between Felix and Flora aloud – and perhaps acting it out, too.

REFLECTIVE LOG

In what ways did acting out the specified section of the script help your written response?

Now, read one student's ideas on how Flora's speeches should be performed.

These lines are addressed to Felix rather than Mercy and establish a number of things about Flora's character – her somewhat patronising way of speaking about Felix, as if he is a child ('boy'), but also the fact that she is upset by her husband's death even if she has got rid of his clothes and bees.

Her tone of voice, however, is probably bitter and sarcastic, and she would emphasise 'clever son' and 'golden boy'. She doesn't really want Felix to 'carry on', as she feels he should have spoken earlier at the service, not now. I think she will say the lines through gritted teeth, to show her anger and frustration.

8. In what ways has the student shown understanding of Flora's character?

9. What aspects of Flora's performance has the student addressed here? Have reasons been given why the actor playing Flora should perform in the way stated?

10. What aspects have *not* been addressed?

11. Choose one of these missing aspects and write a paragraph giving advice to an actor about what to do. Make sure you include reasons for your decisions.

APPLYING THE SKILLS

12. Look at the lines spoken by Mercy from 'Flora! We were just coming in...' to 'Your mother isn't angry with you' (in Unit 6.1). What aspects of Mercy's character would you want to highlight in performance?

CHECKLIST FOR SUCCESS

✓ Include a short, summative statement about Mercy's character, based on the script as a whole, and what we know about her at this point
✓ Comment on tone of voice, facial expression, gestures and movements and anything else you consider relevant in bringing her character to life
✓ Give reasons for your advice

SOUND PROGRESS

• I can write clearly about particular ways in which actors should perform a small section from a script.
• I can write clearly about how a particular aspect such as use of props, costume, set or sound could be used in a longer script.

EXCELLENT PROGRESS

• I can suggest a wide range of ways actors should perform set lines from a script and support my views with detailed understanding of the character.
• I can write in detail, and with relevant dramatic references, about how a particular aspect such as use of props, costume, set or sound could be used effectively in a longer script.

6.3 Writing extended responses

- Consider how to express detailed ideas about acting, design or directorial vision with regard to a longer script

> **SPOTLIGHT ON** How can I write a sustained response on a longer script?

STARTING POINT

It is often relatively easy to select individual moments from a drama and explain what an actor should do, or what prop or lighting design might be appropriate at that point, but it can be more challenging to trace the development of an idea or a character across a longer piece of drama.

Imagine you are an actor playing Felix in *Humble Boy* and have been asked to explain:

- what impression you want the audience to gain of him
- how you want to communicate this meaning.

  1. Jot down your immediate thoughts. Start: 'I want the audience to see that...'

EXPLORING THE SKILLS

Although you have already looked at the script in some detail, this can be hard to answer. Your starting point is to understand and be able to write about the sort of person you believe Felix to be based on the evidence across *the whole* of the script.

  2. What do you think the following evidence suggests about Felix? Reread the script and then copy and complete the table:

Evidence	What this might tell us?
He enters the garden in a 'stumbling, uncertain way'.	It might convey the idea of a 'lost' soul, someone who is unsure where to go. Why might this be? Perhaps because of his father's death.
He is 'transfixed' by the beehive.	The bees were kept by his father, so their removal might seem like another link gone with his father, perhaps even a betrayal?
He's wearing old, greying cricket clothes, even though it is the day of his father's funeral.	

Evidence	What this might tell us?
In the conversation with Mercy, he seems obsessed by the beekeepers who have taken the bees away.	
Even though Mercy tries to encourage him, he ignores her requests to 'come inside'.	
When his mother appears, he speaks to her directly.	
His stammering gets worse when his mother is talking to him.	

3. Once you have completed your table, write a short summary paragraph that conveys what Felix is like as a character. You could start:

It is important to convey to the audience that Felix is clearly hit hard by his father's death. His physical behaviour and what he says, or tries to say, tell us that...

DEVELOPING THE SKILLS

Having analysed the script for evidence, you need to draw on your acting skills to demonstrate how this characterisation will be conveyed. You will need to think about:

- speech – tone of voice, delivery, pace, emphasis
- gesture and movement – posture, facial expression, particular movements
- proxemics – where he might stand or move to within the stage in relation to other characters.

4. Jot down some initial thoughts under each of these headings for Felix. You may find it useful to work with a group to try out your ideas in practice.

Equally important is the idea of change and contrast. When looking at a particular character over the course of a longer piece of drama, you need to consider if there are moments when the character changes or reacts differently.

REFLECTIVE LOG

Think about any of the devised or scripted work you have been involved with. In what ways does any character change over the course of the drama? Make brief notes summing up your ideas.

5. How might Felix change over the course of the script? You could see it as having three phases as in the table below. Copy the table and add some initial notes suggesting how your ideas from trying out acting techniques could be added here – and say why.

Phase 1	Phase 2	Phase 3
Entrance and looking at beehive before Mercy comes in	Mercy's entrance and their conversation	His mother's entrance and their conversation
Acting ideas The stage directions say he is 'transfixed', so as he enters he must keep his eyes on the hive, drawing the audience's attention to it too. He will take the lid off the hive carefully, gingerly, but not in a fearful way.	**Acting ideas**	**Acting ideas**
Rationale The bees have great meaning to him; they are a link to his father, so the way he takes the lid off should be reverential and done with care.	**Rationale**	**Rationale**

6. These three phases are not definitive. You might decide that within each one (or at least some of them) there are further phases. What ways can you see of dividing up the second two phases into further phases?

Compartmentalising the script in this way can be a useful method for actors to visualise the performance, rather like breaking a journey down into a series of smaller trips.

You may also have to look at the script as a whole and consider the overall mood or ideas the playwright wishes to convey.

7. One reviewer of *Humble Boy* called the play 'funny and touching'. Can you identify three moments from the script that might be considered 'touching' – that is, likely to evoke a sympathetic response from the audience?

Once you have decided what these moments are, consider how you could exploit them for maximum impact with the audience. Read this short example from one student:

> I think the moment when Felix has checked the beehive and says, simply, 'The b-b-b-bees have all gone' is very touching and sad. It is the first thing Felix says, and it is about absence – about something that is missing. We find out later that the bees are very important to Felix as they represent his father, perhaps, so he must speak these lines in a very sad, downbeat way. I think once he has verified the bees are no longer there, he could place the lid slowly back on the hive and then move away from it, staring out into the darkness of the sky ask if looking for the bees to return. I think Mercy might move towards him, unseen and reach out a hand as if to touch his shoulder, to comfort him, but then withdraw it just as he turns to face her and say his next line.

8. What particular moment has this student selected? What suggestions has the student come up with to make this moment 'touching'?

9. Do you think these would be effective? Can you think of any other ideas? How could lighting be used at this point?

10. Try out the idea above and any of your own for this moment (you may not be able to use lighting) and evaluate whether or not they created the desired 'touching' effect.

APPLYING THE SKILLS

11. Identify the two other moments from the script which you think are touching and write three or four paragraphs explaining how you would want them to be performed for maximum impact.

CHECKLIST FOR SUCCESS

✓ Make sure you explain what is 'touching' about these moments, and why you have chosen them
✓ Comment in detail on specific suggestions that would give them impact: acting, lighting and so on
✓ Give clear reasons for your choices

SOUND PROGRESS

• I can write at length about a particular approach or development of character in a script.

EXCELLENT PROGRESS

• I can write about creative solutions to match the ideas I wish to convey to the audience.

- Read and respond to an extended script extract
- Evaluate other students' responses

SPOTLIGHT ON

How can I improve my responses to a longer script?

STARTING POINT

The extract you are going to read is taken from English writer John Galsworthy's play, *Strife*, written in 1909. It deals with a strike for better wages and conditions by workers at a factory making tin plate. However, neither the workers, led by a man called Roberts, nor the Chairman and the directors of the company, show any sign of giving in. Enid has gone to visit Mrs Roberts, who used to be a maid for Enid and her father, as she is very unwell.

Characters

ENID UNDERWOOD, daughter of the Chairman, Mr John Anthony

FRANCIS UNDERWOOD, her husband, manager of the tin plate company

DAVID ROBERTS, workers' committee member

ANNIE ROBERTS, his wife

JAN, a boy of 10, son of another worker

This extract is from Act 2, Scene 1. It takes place in Roberts' cottage; Enid has already been there for some time when Roberts returns.

Close to the fireplace in an old armchair, wrapped in a rug, sits Mrs Roberts, a thin and dark-haired woman about thirty-five, with patient eyes. Her hair is not done up, but tied back with a piece of ribbon.

Enid:	*(Very gently.)* I'll get him to talk to me outside, we won't excite you.
Mrs Roberts:	*(Faintly.)* No, M'm.
	(She gives a violent start. Roberts has come in, unseen.)
Roberts:	*(Removing his hat – with subtle mockery.)* Beg pardon for coming in; you're engaged with a lady, I see.
Enid:	Can I speak to you, Mr Roberts?
Roberts:	Whom have I the pleasure of addressing, Ma'am?
Enid:	But surely you know me! I'm Mrs Underwood.
Roberts:	*(With a bow of malice.)* The daughter of our Chairman.

Enid:	*(Earnestly.)* I've come on purpose to speak to you; will you come outside a minute?

She looks at Mrs Roberts.

Roberts:	*(Hanging up his hat.)* I have nothing to say, Ma'am.
Enid:	But I *must* speak to you, please.

She moves towards the door.

Roberts:	*(With sudden venom.)* I have not the time to listen!
Mrs Roberts:	David!
Enid:	Mr Roberts, *please*!
Roberts:	*(Taking off his overcoat.)* I am sorry to disoblige a lady – Mr Anthony's daughter.
Enid:	*(Wavering, then with sudden decision.)* Mr Roberts, I know you've another meeting of the men.
	(Roberts bows.)
	I came to appeal to you. Please, please, try to come to some compromise; give way a little, if it's only for your own sakes!
Roberts:	*(Speaking to himself.)* The daughter of Mr Anthony begs me to give way a little, if it's only for our own sakes.
Enid:	For everybody's sake; for your wife's sake.
Roberts:	For my wife's sake, for everybody's sake – for the sake of Mr Anthony.
Enid:	Why are you so bitter against my father? He has never done anything to you.
Roberts:	Has he not?
Enid:	He can't help his views, any more than you can help yours.
Roberts:	I really didn't know that I had a right to views!
Enid:	He's an old man, and you –

Seeing his eyes fixed on her, she stops.

Roberts:	*(Without raising his voice.)* If I saw Mr Anthony going to die, and I could save him by lifting my hand, I would not lift the little finger of it.
Enid:	You – you – – *(She stops again, biting her lips.)*
Roberts:	I would not, and that's flat!
Enid:	*(Coldly.)* You don't mean what you say, and you know it!
Roberts:	I mean every word of it.
Enid:	But why?
Roberts:	*(With a flash.)* Mr Anthony stands for tyranny! That's why!
Enid:	Nonsense!

Mrs Roberts makes a movement as if to rise, but sinks back in her chair.

Enid:	*(With an impetuous movement.)* Annie!
Roberts:	Please not to touch my wife!
Enid:	*(Recoiling with a sort of horror.)* I believe – you are mad.
Roberts:	The house of a madman then is not the fit place for a lady.

Enid:	I'm not afraid of you.
Roberts:	*(Bowing.)* I would not expect the daughter of Mr Anthony to be afraid. Mr Anthony is not a coward like the rest of them.
Enid:	*(Suddenly.)* I suppose you think it brave, then, to go on with the struggle.
Roberts:	Does Mr Anthony think it brave to fight against women and children? Mr Anthony is a rich man, I believe; does he think it brave to fight against those who haven't a penny? Does he think it brave to set children crying with hunger, an' women shivering with cold?
Enid:	*(Putting up her hand, as though warding off a blow.)* My father is acting on his principles, and you know it!
Roberts:	And so am I!
Enid:	You hate us; and you can't bear to be beaten.
Roberts:	Neither can Mr Anthony, for all that he may say.
Enid:	At any rate you might have pity on your wife.

Mrs Roberts who has her hand pressed to her heart, takes it away, and tries to calm her breathing.

Roberts:	Madam, I have no more to say.

He takes up the loaf. There is a knock at the door, and Underwood comes in. He stands looking at them, Enid turns to him, then seems undecided.

Underwood	Enid!
Roberts:	*(Ironically.)* Ye were not needing to come for your wife, Mr Underwood. We are not rowdies.
Underwood	I know that, Roberts. I hope Mrs Roberts is better. *(Roberts turns away without answering.)* Come, Enid!
Enid:	I make one more appeal to you, Mr Roberts, for the sake of your wife.
Roberts:	*(With polite malice.)* If I might advise ye, Ma'am – make it for the sake of your husband and your father.

Enid, suppressing a retort, goes out. Underwood opens the door for her and follows. Roberts, going to the fire, holds out his hands to the dying glow.

Roberts:	How goes it, my girl? Feeling better, are you?
	(Mrs Roberts smiles faintly. He brings his overcoat and wraps it round her.)
	(Looking at his watch.) Ten minutes to four! *(As though inspired.)* I've seen their faces, there's no fight in them, except for that one old robber.
Mrs Roberts:	Won't you stop and eat, David? You've 'ad nothing all day!
Roberts:	*(Putting his hand to his throat.)* Can't swallow till those old sharks are out o' the town. *(He walks up and down.)* I shall have a bother with the men – there's no heart in them, the cowards. Blind as bats, they are – can't see a day before their noses.
Mrs Roberts:	It's the women, David.

Roberts:	Ah! So they say! They can remember the women when their own bellies speak! The women never stop them from the drink; but from a little suffering to themselves in a sacred cause, the women stop them fast enough.
Mrs Roberts:	But think o' the children, David.
Roberts:	Ah! If they will go breeding themselves for slaves, without a thought o' the future o' them they breed – –
Mrs Roberts:	(Gasping.) That's enough, David; don't begin to talk of that – I won't – I can't –
Roberts:	(Staring at her.) Now, now, my girl!
Mrs Roberts:	(Breathlessly.) No, no, David – I won't!
Roberts:	There, there! Come, come! That's right! (Bitterly.) Not one penny will they put by for a day like this. Not they! Hand to mouth – Gad! – I know them! They've broke my heart. There was no holdin' them at the start, but now the pinch 'as come.
Mrs Roberts:	How can you expect it, David? They're not made of iron.
Roberts:	Expect it? Wouldn't I expect what I would do meself? Wouldn't I starve an' rot rather than give in? What one man can do, another can.
Mrs Roberts:	And the women?
Roberts:	This is not women's work.
Mrs Roberts:	(With a flash of malice.) No, the women may die for all you care. That's their work.
Roberts:	(Averting his eyes.) Who talks of dying? No one will die till we have beaten these – –
	(He meets her eyes again, and again turns his away. Excitedly.)
	This is what I've been waiting for all these months. To get the old robbers down, and send them home again without a farthin's worth o' change. I've seen their faces, I tell you, in the valley of the shadow of defeat.

He goes to the peg and takes down his hat.

Mrs Roberts:	(Following with her eyes – softly.) Take your overcoat, David; it must be bitter cold.
Roberts:	(Coming up to her – his eyes are furtive.) No, no! There, there, stay quiet and warm. I won't be long, my girl!
Mrs Roberts:	(With soft bitterness.) You'd better take it.

She lifts the coat. But Roberts puts it back, and wraps it round her. He tries to meet her eyes, but cannot. Mrs Roberts stays huddled in the coat. Her eyes, that follow him about, are half malicious, half yearning. He looks at his watch again, and turns to go. In the doorway he meets Jan Thomas, a boy of ten in clothes too big for him, carrying a penny whistle.

Roberts:	Hallo, boy!

He goes. Jan stops within a yard of Mrs Roberts, and stares at her without a word.

EXPLORING THE SKILLS

John Galsworthy was writing at a time in Britain when there was increasing conflict between the working classes and their 'betters' (as they were sometimes called) – employers, the aristocracy and so on. At about the same time, other writers were beginning to explore similar issues – for example, George Bernard Shaw in *Pygmalion,* in which a working-class girl is trained to become 'posh'.

Later in the 20th century, playwrights such as John Osborne would write plays in which working-class characters were presented as fully rounded protagonists. As you think about *Strife*, you might want to consider how fully rounded the presentation of Roberts and his wife Annie is.

Answer these questions, based on your reading or performance of the extract:

1. How would you describe the style of the play as it is written? Is it intended to be a realistic drama, fantasy, absurdist, or something else?

2. What are the key themes or ideas that Galsworthy seems to be interested in?

3. What general mood or atmosphere do you think he is trying to achieve?

DEVELOPING THE SKILLS

Now read these more detailed tasks on the extract and the sample responses that follow.

> **Task 1:** In what ways could the costume designer contribute to the realisation of the characters in this extract?

Response A

The play is a realistic one, so I think the characters would dress in the right clothes for the time. The most important thing would be to show the difference between the workers and the rich, so this means the costume designer needs to show shabby poor clothing for Roberts and his wife Annie and have nice clothes for Enid. Roberts says, '...you're engaged with a lady' when he comes in, so it is obvious that she looks different to Annie. Their clothes would be clothes that people wore in the early 20th century, such as for Enid quite fancy embroidery with ribbons. She would definitely wear a dress, probably ankle length and slim-fitting. The audience will see that there is a difference in their lives as Annie would only have cheaper, working-class clothes, probably a plain, single-coloured skirt.

identifies style of play, although a little simplistic

basic contrast but lacking in explanation in relation to play itself

useful direct reference to play

thoughtful but rather general detail, not related to Enid's characterisation

basic detail, lacking development

Comment

This is a clear response, which makes the basic point about the contrast between the working classes and the better off. However, it does not really draw out how costumes could specifically develop characterisation for these particular characters; the suggestions could apply to almost any working-class person and richer woman, not Annie and Enid in particular.

4. How could this response be improved? Think about:

- how the costume design details could be more specific
- how the response could draw on what we find out about the characters.

Response B

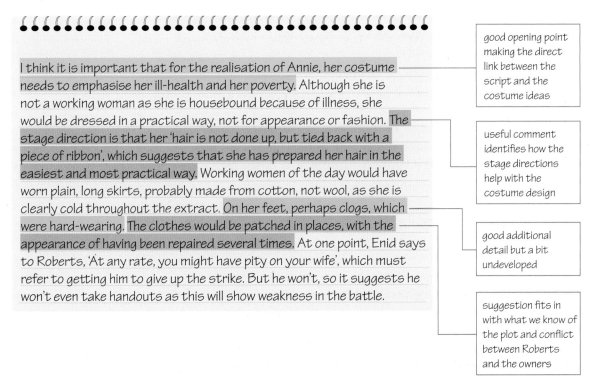

I think it is important that for the realisation of Annie, her costume needs to emphasise her ill-health and her poverty. Although she is not a working woman as she is housebound because of illness, she would be dressed in a practical way, not for appearance or fashion. The stage direction is that her 'hair is not done up, but tied back with a piece of ribbon', which suggests that she has prepared her hair in the easiest and most practical way. Working women of the day would have worn plain, long skirts, probably made from cotton, not wool, as she is clearly cold throughout the extract. On her feet, perhaps clogs, which were hard-wearing. The clothes would be patched in places, with the appearance of having been repaired several times. At one point, Enid says to Roberts, 'At any rate, you might have pity on your wife', which must refer to getting him to give up the strike. But he won't, so it suggests he won't even take handouts as this will show weakness in the battle.

(Annotations:)
- good opening point making the direct link between the script and the costume ideas
- useful comment identifies how the stage directions help with the costume design
- good additional detail but a bit undeveloped
- suggestion fits in with what we know of the plot and conflict between Roberts and the owners

Comment

This is a well-argued response with some detailed, thoughtful ideas based on the text itself. Some further detail on what Annie might or might not be wearing (hat or no hat?) and also how the costume might be used as part of the characterisation (how does Annie interact with what she is wearing?) would help, but this is a solid and helpful response so far.

5. How could this response be improved? Think about:

- how Annie might use her costume to develop her characterisation
- other costume details that have not been mentioned – for example, what else she would be wearing apart from a skirt.

Task 2: Explore the ways in which the role of ROBERTS helps to move the drama along in the extract.

Response A

Roberts is obviously a very important character because he is leader of the workers and the one who is dead against going back to work, even if it means his own family starving. There are quite a few of the other workers who don't completely support him so he is the one who is causing all the problems – you could say he is the one who makes the play exciting. Everything could be ok if Roberts wasn't in the scene as Enid and Annie seem to get along, but Annie knows there will be trouble when he comes back as she gives 'a violent start' when he appears.' This creates tension in the audience and they want to see what will happen between Enid and him.

> a clear point identifying his role in the drama

> this information needs to be supported by direct reference to the text

> there is a good point here, but it is not expressed in a way that shows dramatic knowledge

> good to refer to the dramatic effect but doesn't answer the question directly

Comment

This is a reasonable attempt to try to discuss Roberts' impact, but it does not focus enough on specific moments within the scene, nor express ideas in suitably professional language.

6. How could this be improved? Think about:

- what particular changes happen in the scene as a result of Roberts' words and actions.
- what dramatic function he serves.

Response B

Roberts could be referred to as the antagonist of the play; without him, it could be argued there would be no conflict and therefore no story – the men would simply go back to work. His function is to act as a contrast with Mr Anthony, who is both his opposite and similar in character – he says, 'Mr Anthony is not a coward like the rest of them...' even though he would not 'lift a finger' to save him if he was dying! This suggests that Enid's efforts to calm things are no match for this stubborn man. His main role here is to show how deep the hatred is of his employers, so much that the audience begin to realise his own wife is at risk. When he forbids Enid to help Annie, the audience see that his principles are a sort of madness. It might even be argued that they directly contribute to Annie becoming more unwell, for example when he fails to realise what this is leading to: 'Who talks of dying? No one will die till we have beaten these——'

> identifies Roberts' central role in the play

> evidence from the text supports the point

> shows how his words and actions have a direct impact on audience and developing plot

> good interpretation of character and what it shows in this extract

> refers to his blind pursuit of 'justice'

Comment

This is a strong exploration of Roberts and his general role in the play; a full answer would need to trace in more detail how what he says and does in this scene moves the drama forward.

7. How could this be improved? Think about:

- other ways you could explore Roberts' dramatic role (Is he more of an **archetype** than a realistic character? Why? Why not?)
- how he enables particular themes to be explored and developed.

> **KEY TERMS**
>
> **archetype:** a character that seems to represent a type or category of person (for example, angry working class) rather than a person in their own right

APPLYING THE SKILLS

8. Now it's your turn. Complete this task based on the script:

> **Task 3:** Explore the ways in which the role of ENID helps to move the drama along in the extract.

CHECKLIST FOR SUCCESS

✓ Focus on the extract itself, not on material outside it
✓ Do not waste time retelling what happens
✓ Use appropriate dramatic terms to describe Enid's function and role

SOUND PROGRESS

- I can respond to a longer script identifying and using evidence to support my points in a clear, logical way.

EXCELLENT PROGRESS

- I can respond to a longer script in thoughtful ways that consider its impact on the audience, using fluent expression and appropriate dramatic terminology.

CHECK YOUR PROGRESS

Use these statements as a way of evaluating your progress throughout this chapter.

SOUND PROGRESS ✓

- [ ] I can identify the ways in which characters are different or distinctive and make some basic suggestions about how actors show this in performance.
- [ ] I can write clearly about particular ways in which actors working together should perform a small section from a script.
- [ ] I can write clearly about how a particular aspect such as use of props, costume, set or sound could be used in a longer script.
- [ ] I can write at length about a particular approach or development of character in a script.
- [ ] I can respond to a longer script using evidence to support my points in a clear, logical way.

EXCELLENT PROGRESS ✓

- [ ] I can write clearly and confidently about performances, linking my proposals to the text itself and making relevant inferences from the evidence.
- [ ] I can suggest a wide range of ways actors should perform set lines from a script and support my views with detailed understanding of the character.
- [ ] I can write in detail, and with relevant dramatic references, about how a particular aspect such as use of props, costume, set or sound could be used effectively in a longer script.
- [ ] I can write about creative solutions to match the ideas I wish to convey to the audience.
- [ ] I can respond to a longer script in thoughtful ways that consider its impact on the audience, using fluent expression and appropriate dramatic terminology.

Index

Note: page numbers in **bold** refer to key word definitions.

A

acting skills, development 13–40
  developing convincing roles 14–17
  developing dialogue 26–9
  getting physical 18–21
  using levels/space 30–3
  using your voice 22–5
action 8
  falling 74, 75, 76
  rewinding 77
  rising 74, 75, 76
  variety of 113, 114
alienation 9, **9**
antagonists 140
archetypes 141, **141**
Aristotle 9
articulation 22
atmosphere 53–5, 127
Ayckbourn, Alan, *Invisible Friends* 103

B

back stories 82, 117
Bennett, Alan, *The Madness of George III* 59, 108–15
blocking 46, 48, 106–7, **106**, 114, 117
body language 15, **15**
Brecht, Bertolt 9
Brook, Peter 8

C

catharsis 9, **9**
Chakrabarti, Lolita, *Red Velvet* 35–9
characterisation 27, **27**, 108, 112–13
  and back stories 82
  and costume 60, 138–9
  and extended scripts 124–6, 128–31, 138–9
  and monologues 105–6, 107
  and props 58
  see also roles
characters
  distinctiveness 124
  relationship with others 108
  see also roles

climax 74–6, 93
colour 42–3, 44
  and costume 60, 61, 63
  and emotion 54
  and lighting 53, 54, 55
comedy of the absurd 97
commedia dell'arte 76, **76**, 77
consonants 24, **24**
context 108, 112
contrast 75, **75**, 131, 139–40
costume 42–5, 60–1, 66, 83, 117
  and characterisation 60, 138–9
  colour 60, 61, 63
  style and period 61, 63
  texture 61, 63

D

design and staging 41–68, 90, 91, 114
  costumes 42–5, 60–1, 63, 66
  lighting 43, 44–5, 52–5, 66
  make-up 60, 62–3, 66
  props 44–5, 58–9, 66
  sets 46–51, 65
  sound 43–5, 56–7, 66
devising 69–94
  and communicating meaning 80–3
  and design issues 90, 91
  and effective group work 78–9
  and evaluating and responding 78, 84–7
  and performing 78, 91
  responding to stimuli 70–3, 88–93
  and space 85–6, 90, 92
  structuring devised work 74–7, 78, 90
dialogue 15, **15**, 26–9, 75
directorial concept 43–5, **43**, 90, 92, 93
downstage 46, **46**
drama, definition 7, 8–9
dramatic (narrative) 'arcs' 74–7, 93
Duffy, Carol Ann, *Demeter* 89, 93
Dürrenmatt, Friedrich, *The Visit* 63
dynamics 124, **125**

E

effect 87, 91
Eliot, T S 75

emotion 108, 112–13, 128
empathy 14, **14**, 105
'end on' stages 46–7
enunciation 23, **23**, 24
Euripides, *The Trojan Women* 64–7
exposition 74, 75, 76
extended scripts 119–42

F

facial expression 19, 113–14, 128, 131
flash-forwards 76
flashbacks 76
focus 79
'fourth wall' 47, 85
framing 31
'freeze' the scene technique 28, 31, 113–14
Fresnel 53
frozen tableaux 18–19, **18**, 21, 31–2, 113–14

G

Galsworthy, John, *Strife* 134–41
gels 54
genre 76, **76**, 97, 99–100
gestures 19–20, 24, 28, 38, 83, 117, 128, 131
gobos 53, **53**
'grid', the 52
group work
  effective 78–9
  group discussions 72
  group scripts 108–15

H

Hansberry, Lorraine, *A Raisin in the Sun* 116–17
Hirson, David, *La Bête* 104
hot-seating 16–17, **16**, 106

I

ideas 70–2
  core 125
  evolution 71, **71**
  generation 71–3, 78–9, 88–90
impressionistic 70, **70**
improvisation 72, 76, 96
'in-the-round' performances 48
inflection 22, 27

insight 81, **81**, 104
intention 107–8, 113, 116–17
interpretation 98–101, **98**, 108

Jones, Charlotte, *Humble Boy*
120–33

Kafka, Franz, *The Metamorphosis*
20, 21

language, layout/structure 105
lanterns 52–4
Leigh, Mike 96
levels, using 30–3, 43, 83, 113
lighting 43–5, 52–5, 66, 85
Little Red Riding Hood 44–5, 55
Lorca, Federico García, *The
House of Bernarda Alba* 42–3

make-up **11**, 60, 62–3, 66
mannerisms 28, **28**
'marking the moment' technique
28, 112
meaning 108, 117, 123
communicating 80–3, 130
and nuances 29, **29**
and vocal sounds 23
melodrama, Victorian 97, 99
mime 20, 21
monologues 81, **81**, 102–7, **102**,
116–17
mood 52, 55, 133
motifs 120, **120**, 124
motivation 15
movement 19–21, 28, 38, 83,
114, 117, 125, 131
music 56, 112

note-making 89–90, 120
nuances 29, **29**

onomatopoeic 24, **24**

pace 19, 112
vocal 22, 27, 131
par can 53
parallel scenes 76
performance 78, 91, 95–118, 125

group scripts 108–15
interpretation 98–101
monologues 102–7
repertoires 96–7, 98–101
shaping 81, 112
perspective 49
physicality 113, 114, 117
pitch 22, **23**
plots 108, 112
posture 19, 38, 128, 131
profile lantern 53
promenade performances 48, 86,
86
props 16, 42–5, 58–9, 66, 126–7
Proscenium arch 47
proxemics 30–1, **30**, 83, 113–14,
125, 131
proximity 19
psychological motivations 15
punctuation 22, 105

rake (stage slope) 46, **46**
realism 49, 123, 138
rehearsal 78, 108, 114
reinforcement, positive 79
relationships 30, 108
repertoire 96–7
interpretation 98–101
resolution 74, 75, 76
revenge dramas 97
rewinding action 77
rhythm 19, 105
Ridley, Philip, *Sparkleshark* 29
rigging 52, **52**
rituals 81, **81**
roles
developing convincing 14–17,
80–3, 87, 90, 99–101
dramatic function 140–1
insight into 104
and language 105
preparation 108
see also characterisation;
characters
Rostand, Edmond, *Cyrano de
Bergerac* 99–101
rostra 32, **32**, 33

Sand Burial (play) 32–3
scripts 35–9, 96–7
devising 91
group 108–15

interpretation 99–101
monologues 107
see also extended scripts
sets 43–51, 65
Shaffer, Peter, *Amadeus* 50–1, 59
Shakespeare, William
Hamlet 58, 120
Macbeth 61
Romeo and Juliet 98–9
The Tempest 24, 25, 34–5
shaping performance 81, 112
sound 43, 44–5, 56–7, 66, 112
sound effects 56
soundscapes 57
space 30–3, 85–6, 90, 92
specials 53, 55
spider diagrams 72, 106, 117
stage layouts/configurations
46–51, **46**, 66–7, 85, 114
staging *see* design and staging
Stanislavski, Konstantin 15
stimuli, responding to 70–3,
88–93
'street' scenes 57
subtext 108, **108**
syllables 22, **23**, 24
System, The 15, **15**

'temperature' 55
tempo, vocal 22
theatre, definition 7, 10–11
'thrust' configuration 47
tragedy 9, 61, 97, 99
traverse stage 48, 67

upstage 46, **46**

Victorian melodrama 97, 99
voice 22–5, 38, 117
exploring sound through 56
punctuation 22, 105
stress 22, 24, 128, 131
tone of 117, 128–9, 131
Voznesensky, Andrei, *First Frost*
72–3, 74

words 23–4

Williams, Tennessee, *A Streetcar
Named Desire* 54–5, 57
words 23–4